THE UNOFFICIAL POKÉMON GO FIELD GUIDE

From the Editors of Tips & Tricks Magazine

ISBN-10: 1-942556-56-5
ISBN-13: 978-1-942556-56-5

Printed in the U.S.A.

Photo Credits: Acorn 1/Alamy: p185; Asia File/Alamy: p98; DPA Picture Alliance/Alamy: p176; DuneBug/Stockimo/Alamy: p175; Menelao Michalatos/Alamy: p178; Michael Kemp/Alamy: p190; Pacific Press/Alamy: p193; PhotoStock-Israel/Alamy: p188; Wenn Ltd/Alamy: p199; ZumaPress/Alamy: p179, 198. Charlotte Elsom/Rex/Shutterstock/AP Images: p194, 197; Hitoshi Yamada/NurPhoto/AP Images: p196; Matt Sayles/Invision/AP Images: p201; S Meddle/ITV/Rex/Shutterstock/AP Images: p201; XPX/Star Max/IPX/AP Images: p200. Everett Collection: p186, 189. Shutterstock: p170. Courtesy Pokematch/RenualSoftware B.V.: p192. Juan Zielaskowski/Topix Media Lab: p114, 116, 117, 118, 119.
All other photography © Topix Media Lab
All screenshots © Niantic, Inc.

Published by Media Lab Books
14 Wall Street, Suite 4B
New York, NY 10005

CEO Tony Romando

Vice President of Brand Marketing Joy Bomba
Director of Finance Vandana Patel
Director of Sales and New Markets Tom Mifsud
Manufacturing Director Nancy Puskuldjian
Junior Analyst Matthew Quinn

Editor-in-Chief Jeff Ashworth
Creative Director Steven Charny
Photo Director Dave Weiss
Managing Editor Courtney Kerrigan
Senior Editor Tim Baker

Content Editor James Ellis
Content Designer Michelle Lock
Content Photo Editor Lindsay Pogash
Art Director Susan Dazzo
Assistant Managing Editor Holland Baker
Photo Editor Meg Reinhardt
Designer Danielle Santucci
Assistant Editors Trevor Courneen, Alicia Kort, Kaytie Norman
Contributing Writer Casey Halter
Contributing Photo Editor Evander Batson
Editorial Assistants Liam Baker, Claire Grant, Amanda Jaguden, Abigail Kosisko, Anna Langston
Design Assistants Yerin Kim, Juan Zielaskowski

Co-Founders Bob Lee, Tony Romando

THE UNOFFICIAL Pokémon GO FIELD GUIDE

Of the millions of players chasing Charmanders and pursuing Pikachus around the world, a select few have set themselves apart as the world's best. I'm journalist Ivy St. Ive, and while my passion for all things Pokémon might lead you to believe I was raised by a colony of wild Golbats, I grew up like most of you did—in love with the video games, cartoons, movies and everything else Pokémon. So when Pokémon Go offered me a chance to live out my decades-long dream of becoming a real-life Ash Ketchum, I threw myself into this new alternate reality like a Clefairy at a giant moonstone and managed to become one of the country's first professional pokémon trainers. My story has been featured by media outlets, such as *The New York Times*, NBC, the BBC, BuzzFeed and more. Thus far, I've been more than happy to share whatever tips I can with fellow trainers and pokémon enthusiasts around the world, but I haven't yet had the opportunity to share the full breadth of my knowledge—until now. This Field Guide provides me with the space to divulge every tactic, strategy and shortcut I've learned in the game thus far. With it, I'll teach you how to become a legend among your fellow trainers, no matter what level you're at right now. So read on—your path to Pokémon Go greatness awaits.

Ivy St. Ive

—Ivy St. Ive
Pokémon Master Trainer

TABLE OF CONTENTS

POKÉMON GLOSSARY

The terms you need to know in order to become a Pokémon master.

AUGMENTED REALITY (AR) (1)

A live view of your physical environment, for example a street you're standing on, with superimposed computer-generated images, audio and graphics.

BATTLE

When you go to a rival gym or defend your own, you release the pokémon of your choice and have it rumble with other pokémon.

CANDY

You can get candies by catching pokémon, hatching eggs or by transferring pokémon to Professor Willow. Giving candies to your pokémon can strengthen or evolve them.

CP (COMBAT POWER)

Pokémon have a certain amount of CP when they are first captured. Generally the higher the CP stat, the better they are in battle. The max number of CP a pokémon can have is dependent on trainer level and the specific species of pokémon.

DEFENDER BONUS

For joining a gym and leaving one of your pokémon to defend it, a player will get stardust and pokécoins as a daily reward. Players can reap this reward at the pokéshop.

EGGS

Pokémon eggs are found at pokéstops and can be granted when you level up. They can be hatched into pokémon, though you will have to do some walking first.

EVOLUTION

By giving your pokémon enough candies, they can evolve into stronger, rarer and more powerful pokémon.

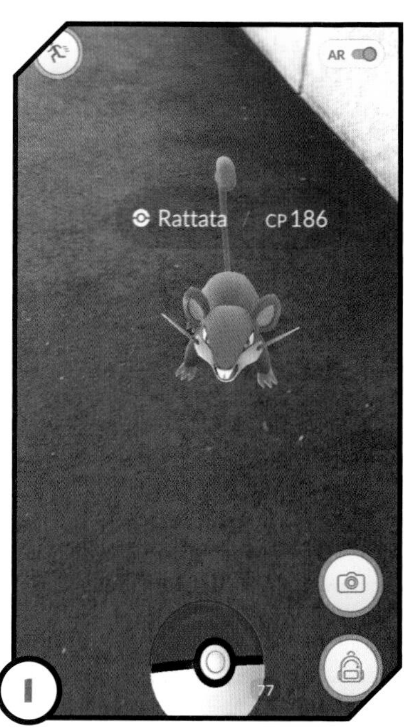

GYMS

Allied gyms are controlled by members of your team. Rival gyms are controlled by members of other teams. In allied gyms, you can train your pokémon for XP and help teammates defend their spots. In rival gyms, you battle your pokémon for XP and control of the gym.

HP (HIT POINTS)

Hit points measure your pokémon's health. If your pokémon runs out of HP, it faints and can't fight until it's revived.

INCENSE

You can use incense, which you can buy at the shop or find at pokéstops, to attract pokémon to your avatar.

INCUBATOR

If you want to hatch an egg that you've collected, place it in the incubator. After you walk a certain distance with the app open, the incubated egg will hatch, adding a new pokémon to your collection.

INDIVIDUAL VALUES (IV)

In Pokémon Go, there are three hidden stats or "individual values" that affect how strong pokémon are in gym battles. They are Attack, Defense and Stamina. These "IV scores" affect both the species as a whole and individual pokémon.

LEVELS

Every trainer starts off at Level 1, but as they gather XP by catching pokémon, evolving them, visiting pokéstops and battling at gyms they can advance to higher levels. When a trainer reaches a new level, they automatically receive rewards and also attract stronger, rarer pokémon. This can help their pokémon achieve higher CP scores.

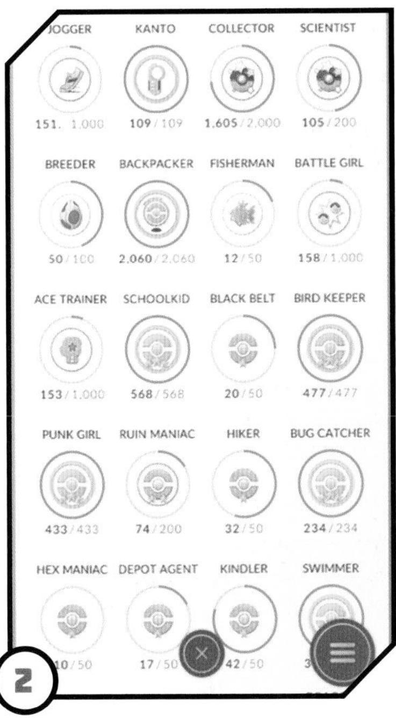

LUCKY EGG

By using a lucky egg, you can double the number of XP you earn for 30 minutes, meaning you're the one who is actually lucky when you snag this item!

LURE MODULE

You can set up a lure module, which you can purchase at the shop or earn through leveling up. Activate one at a pokéstop, and it will bring pokémon near that stop for 30 minutes. Anyone can see and use your lure to their own advantage.

MEDALS (2)

You're awarded medals throughout the game for various achievements, including collecting a set number of specific pokémon types or for walking certain distances.

POKÉMON

These are the creatures who are dominating your every waking moment. The name pokémon is a play on the phrase "pocket monster," which is what they are!

POKÉBALL

An item used to catch and contain pokémon. You can find more pokéballs at pokéstops or purchase them with pokécoins. You can also get the great ball and ultra ball after reaching certain levels, which are each a step up from pokéballs and can capture stronger pokémon.

POKÉCOINS (3)

Pokémon Go's currency, with which you can purchase premium items. To get pokécoins, buy them in the shop with real money or earn them by controlling gyms.

POKÉDEX

You can view all of the pokémon species you have caught and their stats in this pokémon index.

POKÉSTOP (4)

A pokéstop is where you can collect free goods, such as eggs, potions, incubators and pokéballs. Pokéstops are usually placed in prominent public places, like train stations, churches and landmarks.

POTIONS

You feed potions to your pokémon to heal them and restore their HP.

POWER-UP

In order to make your pokémon more effective fighters in battle, trainers can use stardust and candy to up their pokémon's HP and CP.

PRESTIGE

As more allies train and win at a gym, the gym earns more prestige, allowing it to level up and add more defenders, making it harder to capture.

RAZZ BERRY (5)

By feeding this to a pokémon during an encounter, it will be easier to catch and less likely to run away.

REVIVE

If your pokémon faints during a battle, it needs to be brought back to life with a revive, which you can start collecting after you reach Level 5.

STARDUST

Stardust is used to power up pokémon. You can earn stardust by catching pokémon, hatching eggs or by protecting or training at a gym.

TRAINERS

The people who play Pokémon Go.

TRAINING

You can train your pokémon one at a time for XP in allied gyms against the pokémon of other players who also belong to your team.

TYPES

All pokémon have one or two fighting types, such as psychic or water, that have strengths and weaknesses against other pokémon types. Using knowledge about types, trainers are able to strategize against opponents in battles.

XP (EXPERIENCE POINTS) (6)

Experience points measure your progress as a trainer. If you hit a certain amount of XP, you will level up.

POWER UP YOUR PHONE

How to optimize your cell to improve battery life and keep the app from crashing. No stardust required.

Like many new apps, Pokémon Go is prone to crashing often and draining your battery life quicker than a Jolteon's Thunder Shock attack. Hopefully future updates of the app will address some of these problems. Until then, these tricks should help your screen from freezing right before you catch that Growlithe.

HOW TO KEEP YOUR PHONE FROM CRASHING

GENERAL TIPS

- Restart your phone before starting a play session.
- Relog into your Google Account, and then restart the app.
- Restart the app whenever it freezes or whenever the gym freezes. Users have also reported that restarting periodically can be beneficial because it helps the game load.
- Turn off Music and Sounds.
- Make sure you're playing with a strong Wi-Fi or 4G connection.
- Turn off the AR camera (found in the upper-right-hand corner of the screen).
- Close out all other apps while playing Pokémon Go.

FOR IPHONE

- Update to the latest version of iOS.
- Go to Settings > General > Background App Refresh and make sure it is turned off.
- Go to Settings > General > Siri and make sure it is turned off.
- Go to Settings > Privacy > Camera > Pokémon Go and make sure it is turned off.
- Go to Settings > Display & Brightness to turn off Auto-Brightness.
- Clear your RAM: Close all applications. On the home screen, hold down the Power button until the shutdown screen appears. Then hold down the Home button until the shutdown screen disappears.
- Completely close out Pokémon Go by double clicking the home button and swiping the app up. Turn on Airplane Mode, then open the app again. When you see a red bar that says "No Wi-Fi," swipe up from the bottom of your screen to open the Control Center and turn off Airplane mode/turn on Wi-Fi.

HOW TO SAVE YOUR PHONE'S BATTERY

Because you need to have the app open in order to locate nearby pokémon and log kms for hatching eggs, Pokémon Go will drain your battery like no other app. While having a back-up power source and a charger on you is ideal, here are some other tips to conserve battery power.

WITHIN POKÉMON GO

- Go to Settings and turn off Music.
- Go to Settings and turn off Augmented Reality Mode.
- To passively play the game, tap the pokéball, then the top right settings. Turn your phone upside down, then activate the battery saver mode. The screen will turn off but everything else still runs. Just hold onto your phone with earphones in and it will make a sound when a pokémon is near.

GENERAL PHONE TIPS

- Turn the brightness as low as possible while still being able to see the screen.
- Turn off Wi-Fi so your phone isn't searching for a signal.
- Find large public areas with free Wi-Fi to play, such as a mall or park.

SAVING YOUR DATA

Keep Pokémon Go from consuming a month's worth of data in one afternoon.

TO DO THIS

- Open Google Maps on your phone
- Tap the menu button
- Navigate to the Settings menu
- Tap on "Offline areas"
- Tap on the recommended "Home" region or use the "+" button in the bottom-right-hand corner to select a specific area of the map, and then download.

EXPERT ADVICE

Pokémon hunting around tall buildings or skyscrapers can cause your phone's GPS signal to "bounce," tricking the game into thinking you're constantly moving when you aren't. This can help with hatching eggs, but it may take trial and error.

Turning off AR, or augmented reality, when catching wild pokémon can save your phone's battery, as well as save you frustration.

MAXIMIZING YOUR GEAR

Making the most out of Pokémon Go's items.

INCENSE

Activating an incense will attract pokémon to you, wherever you are, for 30 minutes. It can be used while stationary or while you're on the go, and it will make you more likely to attract rarer or higher-level pokémon than you'd normally find in the game. However, because they only really attract around one additional pokémon per minute while still, **we recommend using this item in tandem with a lure module or while on the go visiting pokéstops** (which also tend to attract more pokémon) than simply using incense alone.

LURE MODULE

This item can only be activated at pokéstops and will attract pokémon to a singular location for 30 minutes. Lure modules benefit every player in an area and tend to breed a community environment wherever you put one down. For maximum efficiency with this item, **organize a "lure party" with a few friends and take turns putting lures down at a pre-planned location.** If you get enough people involved, you can make all the pokémon come to you for hours without having to move from one location to another.

LUCKY EGGS

Special eggs that double your XP for 30 minutes when activated, the most efficient use for a lucky egg is to **save it for a time when you are about to evolve a lot of pokémon.** Each evolution earns you 500 XP, one of the highest XP boosts in the game, and when you evolve with a lucky egg, you double that already considerable sum. Often, players will save up dozens of pokémon and evolve them all at one time as a quick way to move up levels.

EXPERT ADVICE

Niantic has officially hinted that pokéstops may soon serve as healing centers for battle-worn monsters, an homage to the original series' pokécenters. This change will be essential for pokémon battle masters, who are already complaining that the number of potions doled out in the game is far too little to maintain long-term fighting.

RAZZ BERRIES

Feeding a pokémon a Razz Berry before throwing a pokéball to capture it will make it about 5 to 10 percent less likely to run away if your throw misses or if the pokémon breaks free. You can feed a Razz Berry to a pokémon before every throw, so feel free to **provide any extra-special pokémon a real feast if you want the best odds of adding them to your collection.**

POTIONS/SUPER POTIONS/ HYPER POTIONS

You can only get these items from walking to pokéstops, so if you plan on battling in gyms a lot, walk around and stock up first. **Once you reach a higher level, don't expect normal potions to aid**

One of the puzzles of Pokémon Go is figuring out a balance of materials that your trainer carries along with them on their journey. Specific combinations of balls, potions, lures and eggs vary by trainer.

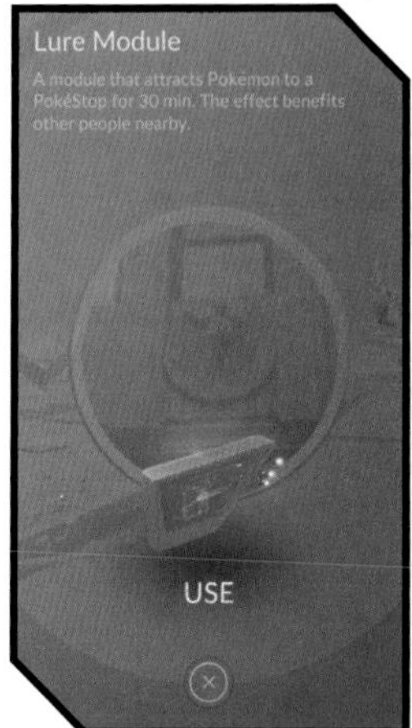

your pokémon as much. Super Potions and Hyper Potions are what you're really going to want to focus on.

POKÉ/GREAT/ULTRA BALLS

You'll notice when you switch from a normal pokéball to a great or ultra ball that the color surrounding a pokémon's capture zone may change, dropping down a difficulty level for instance, from red to orange or from orange to yellow. This is in-game feedback reassuring you the pokémon will now be easier to capture. **If you're having a hard time catching a pokémon, try switching to a great ball first to see if that knocks the capture zone to an acceptable shade** before unleashing your precious ultra balls.

REVIVES

You'll only use these if your pokémon faints in a battle or after you've stationed a pokémon at a gym and it has been knocked out of the lineup. For this reason, you're probably going to be using revives far less than potions. **If you need extra space for pokéballs or potions, we recommend deleting revives first.** To do so, just hit the garbage can icon on the right side of the item and select how many you'd like to do away with.

EGG INCUBATORS

You are given one unlimited egg incubator at the start of the game and intermittently receive incubators (which can only be used three times each) at pokéstops or as you level up in the game (see page 114 for more info on what you receive as you level up). **We recommend saving your three-time-use incubators for more difficult 10km or 5km eggs** (which hatch rarer, more high level pokémon) and saving your unlimited incubator to hatch easier 2km eggs (which often hatch common pokémon). No one wants to spend a hard-earned incubator on hatching yet another Rattata.

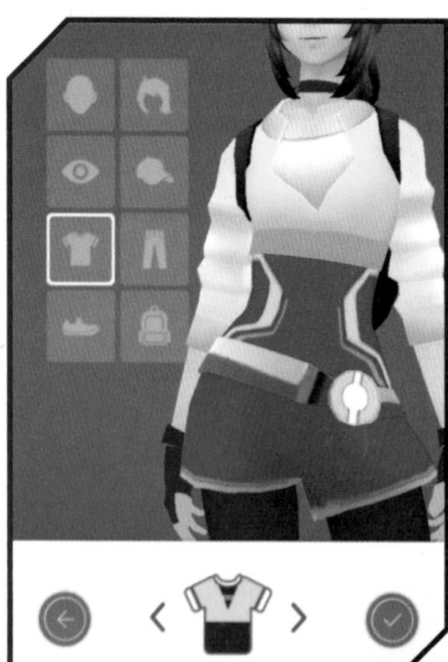

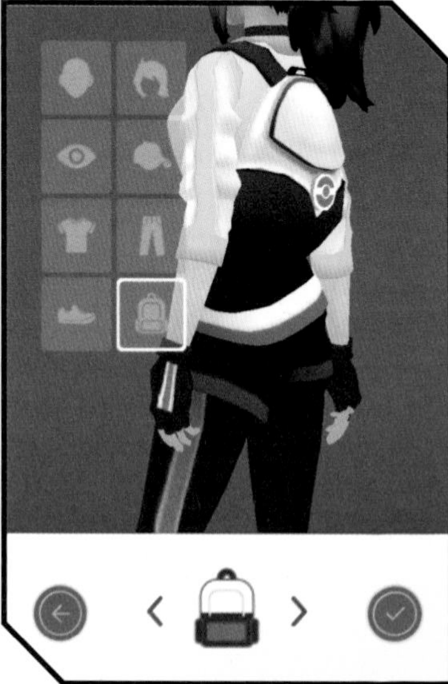

Customizing your avatar is your introduction to the pokémon universe, and the game makes it very easy to get lost in the number of combinations available to potential pokémasters. Facial appearance, general style, clothing and body type can all be personalized.

DIVING IN

How to maximize your first steps down the path to pokémon mastery.

One of your first choices in the game will be between Squirtle, Bulbasaur and Charmander, but Pikachu is also in reach with a little ingenuity.

GETTING STARTED

The first decision you make in Pokémon Go is what the avatar that represents you in the digital realm will look like. Don't worry too much about picking hair color, eye color or your trainer outfit. You can always go back and change them later on in the game by clicking on your profile page. Once you're finished designing your avatar, you'll see it dropped into a map of your surrounding area. This screen will be your main area for finding pokémon, pokéstops, gyms and everything else you've been hearing so much about. But before you can get overwhelmed by this brand new world, Professor Willow explains some basics, like how to throw a pokéball, and helps you capture your first pokémon. Three pokémon will pop up near your location on the map—a Charmander, Bulbasaur and Squirtle—and if you tap on one of them, you'll switch from the map to the screen where you're in a one-on-one confrontation with a pokémon. You'll need to use this opportunity to learn how to throw your pokéball accurately because in the wild, pokémon can escape the ball and run away.

EXPERT ADVICE

Pokémon "nests," or places where rare types regularly spawn, are liable to change every few weeks. Know that your prime Dratini fishing site may soon be overrun with Eevees, so act fast!

At the bottom of your screen is a pokéball. Tap and hold that pokéball with your finger. Now you'll see a white ring surrounding the pokémon, along with a green-, yellow-, orange- or red-colored ring that repeatedly shrinks. Your aim is to throw the pokéball at the colored ring in front of each pokémon. If you hit the circle at its widest, you'll get a 10 XP bonus after you capture it. If you hit the circle when it has shrunk down to exactly

Pokémon aren't very discerning with regards to where they pop up. That could mean the bathroom, a business meeting or even on top of your dog.

EXPERT ADVICE

In your pokémon tracking chart, pokémon will appear in order from closest to farthest. Though exact distances have yet to be determined for what this chart means, know that if a pokémon appears in your feed, it's likely to be only a few city blocks away.

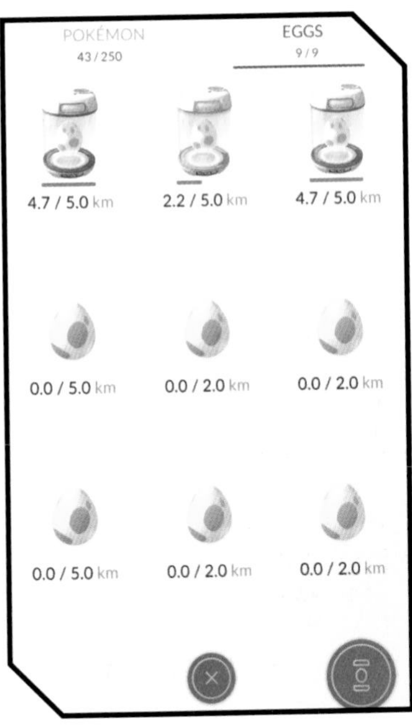

Eggs can be hatched in Pokémon Go by walking in the real world, an exercise incentive that some players have unsuccessfully tried to bypass with tricks. We reveal on page 168.

50 percent, you'll get a 50 XP bonus. If you hit the circle at its smallest, you will be awarded a 100 XP bonus. Throwing a curveball by spinning the pokéball can also fetch you an additional 10 XP if you catch the pokémon. This technique is at first difficult to master but is worth the effort to learn because it'll help you level up faster and catch pokémon more easily than just about anything else.

GETTING STRONGER

Now that you have your first pokémon in your pokédex, it's time to start exploring and gaining some XP. When you look back at the map, you'll notice that you're staring down at your neighborhood. The app uses GPS tracking and Google Maps to place the pokémon in your world, which is why you are seeing all of these cute critters hanging out at restaurants and city hall buildings in all your social media feeds.

Although much of the game's fun comes from spotting pokémon at your workplace or hopping around your kitchen, you can click the "AR" button in the top right hand corner to turn your camera off and replace the real world background with a generic, cartoon one, which saves your phone battery. Changing out of AR mode also makes it easier for you to catch flying pokémon like Zubats. The mechanics

EXPERT ADVICE

Pokémon get harder and harder to catch the more you level up in the game. Experience points needed to level up also increase exponentially at higher trainer levels. If you're hoping to get really good, expect the game to get a lot more difficult.

of capturing a pokémon stay the same in or out of AR mode—if anything, it can be a little bit easier.

You also have probably noticed the item in your inventory called an incubator. This becomes useful once you acquire an egg, which you can randomly receive from a pokéstop. When you place an egg in an incubator, the game starts tracking how much you walk. When you reach a certain distance, the egg hatches into a pokémon. Eggs come in three different varieties based on their hatching distance—2 kilometers, 5

From left: Public parks, especially those with easily identifiable signage and a lot of foot traffic, are often locations for pokéstops; a Golbat prepares to get an infusion of stardust, making it that much more powerful.

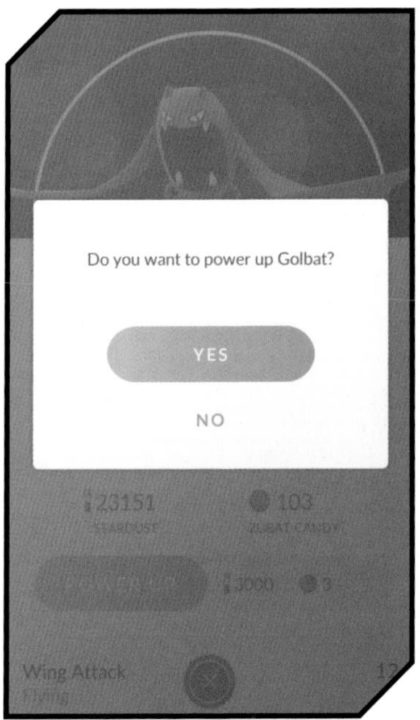

kilometers and 10 kilometers. As you probably guessed, the greater the distance, the rarer and better the pokémon that hatches.

POINTS OF INTEREST

Nabbing your first pokémon is an unforgettable—and addictive—experience. So now that you've gotten a taste, get out there and start catching all 151 of them! Silhouettes of nearby pokémon will appear at the bottom of your screen, so if you walk around the block, you might just be able to catch them. You'll also see several giant blue squares on the map. These are pokéstops and have been placed by the game at general points of interest. Click on these and start spinning the circle that appears with your finger to get all sorts of items, from additional pokéballs to potions (which can heal your pokémon) and more.

ENHANCING YOUR POKÉMON

You've probably noticed by now that when you capture a wild pokémon, you receive stardust and candy.

Stardust can be used on any pokémon to upgrade their HP and CP. Candy is specific to each pokémon species. Once you've acquired enough candies for a particular species of pokémon, you can spend those candies on a pokémon to evolve it to a stronger form. Each pokémon comes with three pieces of candy attached to them when caught

Great throws may yield bonus XP, but you'll still receive three pieces of candies regardless.

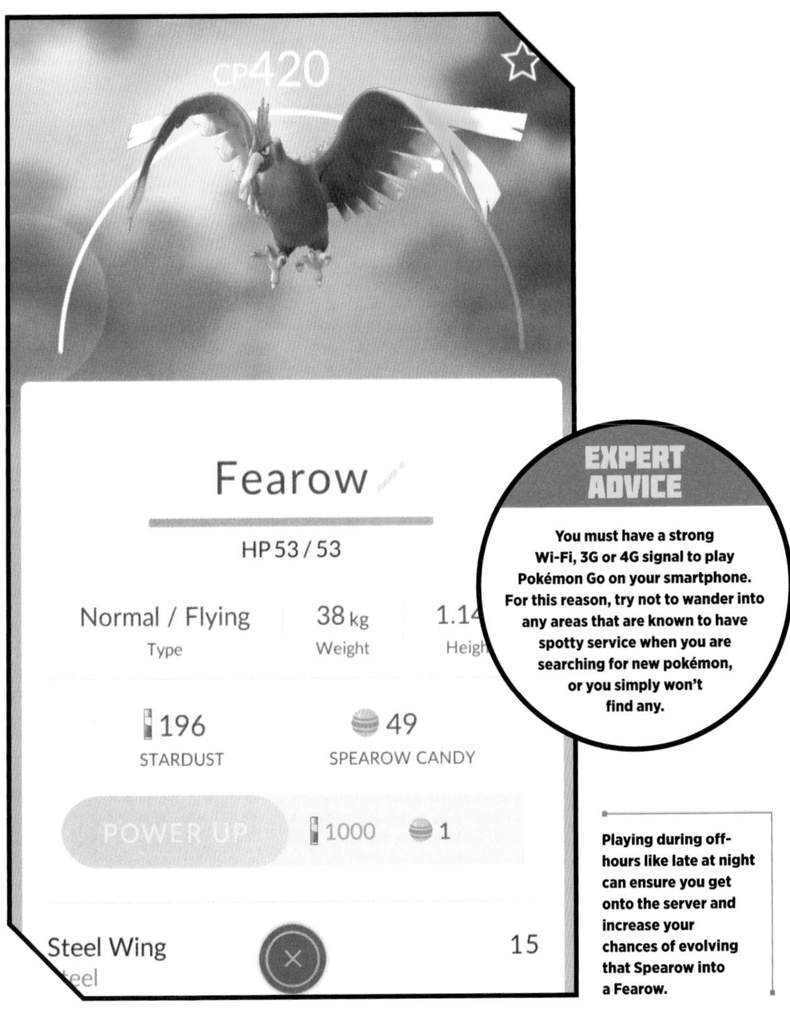

EXPERT ADVICE

You must have a strong Wi-Fi, 3G or 4G signal to play Pokémon Go on your smartphone. For this reason, try not to wander into any areas that are known to have spotty service when you are searching for new pokémon, or you simply won't find any.

Playing during off-hours like late at night can ensure you get onto the server and increase your chances of evolving that Spearow into a Fearow.

in the wild. You can also get 1 piece of candy by transferring extra pokémon to the Professor.

Evolved pokémon are vital additions to your collection if you want to compete in the gym battles that open up once your trainer levels up. But first, you need to be familiar with Pokémon Go's stable of monsters. And we've got you covered....

CP688
Poliwrath
CP551
Rhydon
CP688
Seadra
CP767
Scyther
CP431
Tangela
CP147
Cubone
CP118
Electabuzz
CP52
Charmander
CP896
Exeggutor
CP482
Nidorina
CP79
Onix
CP239
Slowpoke
CP407
Magmar
CP11
Pikachu
CP394
Nidoqueen
CP187
Tauros
CP516
Vileplume
CP28
Chansey
Vaporeon
CP145
Dewgong
CP1127
Dragonite
CP192
Pidgey
CP10
Vulpix
CP549
Electrode
CP470
Fearow

THE COMPLETE POKÉPEDIA

The secrets behind all 151 of the game's elusive monsters are finally revealed—including how to catch them!

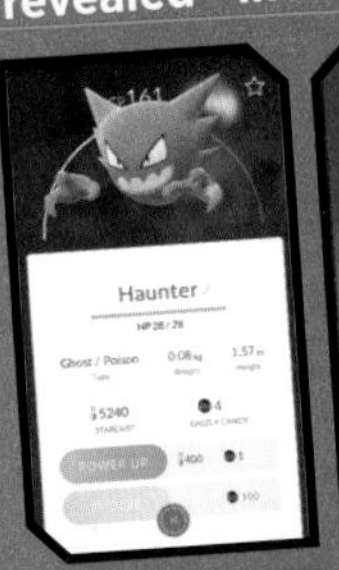

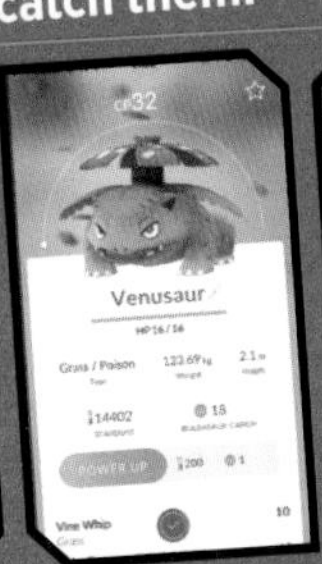

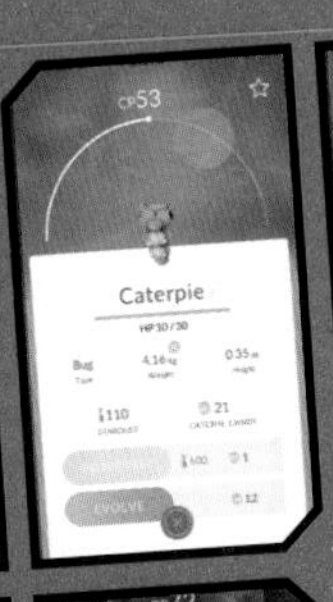

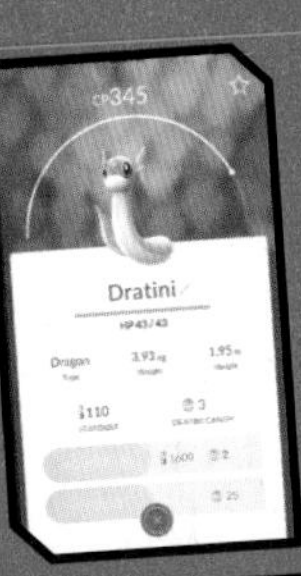

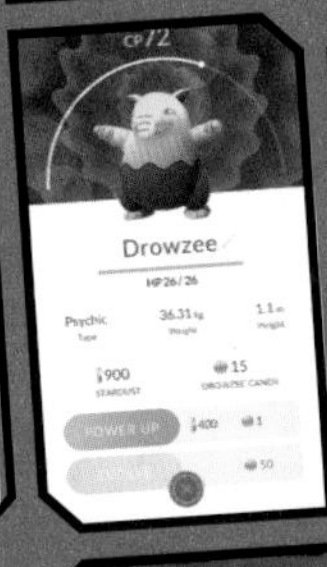

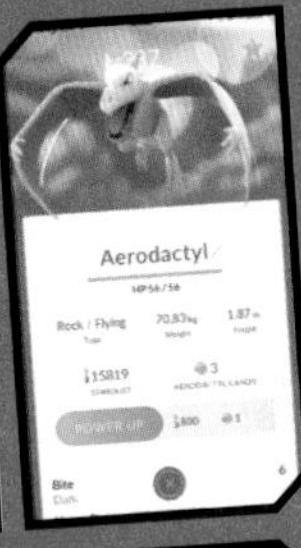

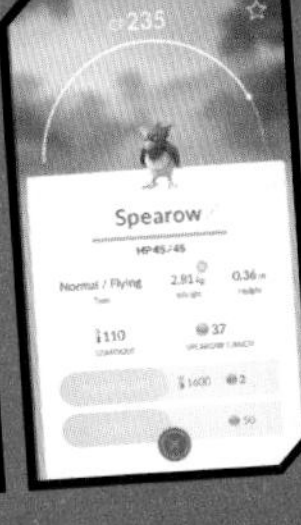

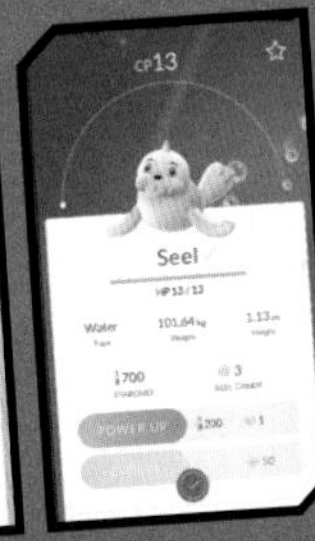

#001 BULBASAUR

CLASSIFICATION Seed pokémon
TYPE Grass/Poison

This small green quadruped is available to trainers as one of three starter pokemon. Its attacks can include Vine Whip, Tackle, Power Whip, Seed Bomb and Sludge Bomb. After receiving 25 Bulbasaur candies, the small green bud on its back begins to flower, transforming it into Ivysaur. After receiving 100 more candies, the flower blooms, causing its final evolution into Venusaur.

EXPERT ADVICE

Try searching for Bulbasaur in grassy areas, like golf courses or playing fields in your neighborhood. They can be quite common in the wild, but only if you know where to look.

#002 IVYSAUR

CLASSIFICATION Seed pokémon
TYPE Grass/Poison

The flower Ivysaur carries on its back is the main source of its poison protection, but its pointed teeth and heftier build also make it a strong battler, especially when compared to its pre-evolved form, Bulbasaur. Reminiscent of an aquamarine, herbivorous dinosaur, Ivysaur may stock some special pre-historic attacks, including Razor Leaf and Solar Beam. Power Whip and Sludge Bomb may also sit in its roster.

EXPERT ADVICE

Ivysaur is both rare in the wild and very difficult to catch once you find it. The most sure-fire way to add one to your pokédex is by evolving Bulbasaur, which seems to be far more common.

#003 VENUSAUR

CLASSIFICATION Seed pokémon
TYPE Grass/poison

Venusaur absorbs energy from the sun and channels that energy directly in a battle. As the final form of Bulbasaur, this pokémon is one of the strongest grass types in the game. Use it against ground-, rock- and water-type pokémon.

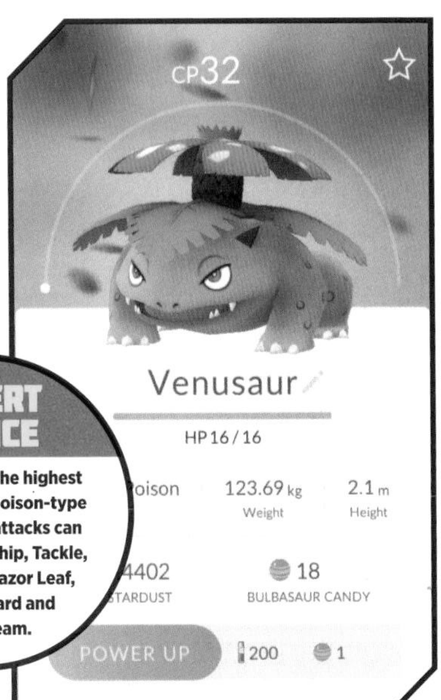

EXPERT ADVICE

Venusaur has the highest defense of all poison-type pokémon. Its attacks can include Vine Whip, Tackle, Take Down, Razor Leaf, Petal Blizzard and Solar Beam.

#004 CHARMANDER

CLASSIFICATION Lizard pokémon
TYPE Fire

Legend has it that the ember burning on the end of Charmander's tail is its main life force, and that this pokémon will die if the flame ever goes out. The pokémon's affinity for flame shows in its possible attacks, all of which are fire type except for Scratch, a normal-type attack. A Charmander will evolve into Charmeleon after receiving 25 Charmander candies.

EXPERT ADVICE

Charmander is one of three pokémon you can choose from as your starter pokémon. He might be your best bet, as fire pokémon seem to be rarer in many areas than other types of pokémon.

#005 CHARMELEON

CLASSIFICATION Flame pokémon
TYPE Fire

This intermediary evolution is a strong fire-type contender in gym battles. While nowhere near the powerhouse of Charizard, Charmeleon still makes for a potent threat against pokémon weak to fire types, such as ice types and grass types. Charmeleon will evolve into a Charizard after receiving 100 Charmander candies.

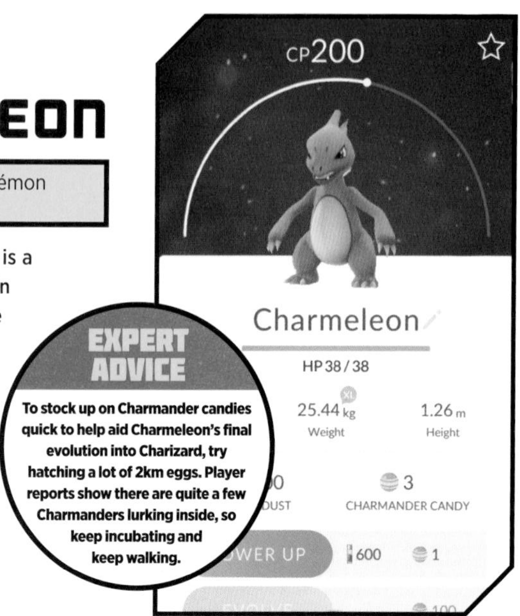

EXPERT ADVICE

To stock up on Charmander candies quick to help aid Charmeleon's final evolution into Charizard, try hatching a lot of 2km eggs. Player reports show there are quite a few Charmanders lurking inside, so keep incubating and keep walking.

#006 CHARIZARD

CLASSIFICATION Flame pokémon
TYPE Fire/Flying

Charizard is the quintessential fully evolved basic pokémon. When pictured in AR mode, it can stand as tall as many humans and can fight with its claws, fangs and wings to evade capture. Long-known as the mascot of "Pokémon Red," Charizard packs a wide array of special fire attacks and can also harness power from the sun to make his damaging flames even harsher in battle.

EXPERT ADVICE

Charizard is very rare in the game so far, but has been lured by players using incense, which often attracts rarer and stronger pokémon. You may also find one at the beach or in dry climates if you're lucky.

#007 SQUIRTLE

CLASSIFICATION Tiny Turtle pokémon
TYPE Water

In the Pokémon universe, Squirtle is a tiny turtle that uses its shell to protect itself and keep it afloat while swimming. It is one of the three starter pokémon you can choose from in the beginning of Pokémon Go, and it has the ability to spray water out of its mouth in a battle to disarm opponents and dole out damage. After 25 Squirtle candies, it evolves into Wartortle.

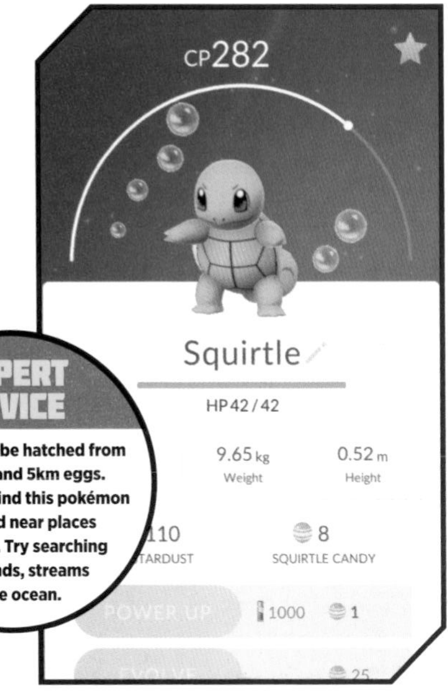

EXPERT ADVICE

Squirtles can be hatched from both 2km and 5km eggs. You can also find this pokémon in the wild near places with water. Try searching near ponds, streams or the ocean.

#008 WARTORTLE

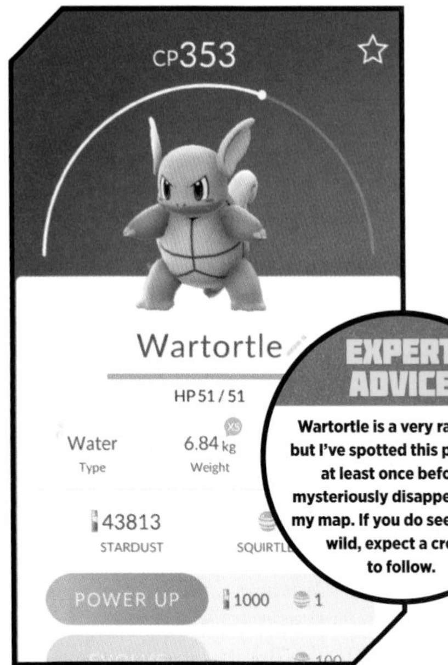

CLASSIFICATION Turtle pokémon
TYPE Water

Wartortle uses its fur-covered tail and ears to store air underwater and propel itself with bubbles, enabling it to swim at super-fast speeds, according to Pokémon lore. This intermediary evolution between Squirtle and Blastoise requires 100 additional Squirtle candies to reach its final form. Its attacks in battle are common to other water-types and can include Bite, Aqua Jet, Water Pulse and Hydro Pump.

EXPERT ADVICE

Wartortle is a very rare find, but I've spotted this pokémon at least once before it mysteriously disappeared off my map. If you do see it in the wild, expect a crowd to follow.

#009 BLASTOISE

CLASSIFICATION Shellfish pokémon
TYPE Water

Using the massive guns located on both sides of its shell, Blastoise is able to blow away its competition with a wide array of powerful water attacks. One of the most recognizable pokémon in the world thanks to its status as the mascot of the original "Pokémon Blue," Blastoise continues its domination in augmented reality. Its most powerful attack by far is Hydro Pump, followed by Ice Beam.

EXPERT ADVICE

It may be better to capture a Blastoise through evolution, rather than catching it in the wild, as player reports so far have shown that Blastoise are often very weak when found out in the world.

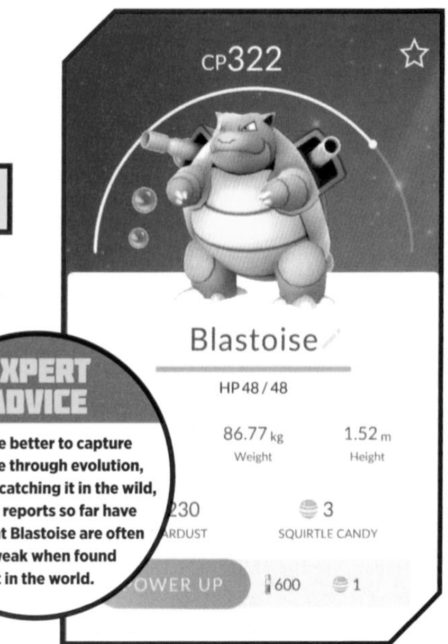

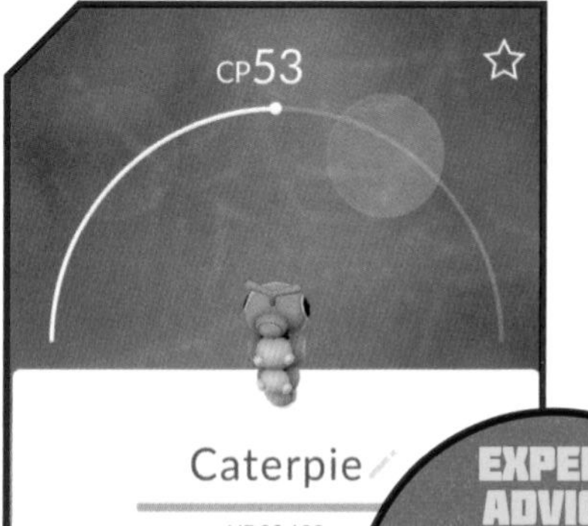

#010 CATERPIE

CLASSIFICATION Worm pokémon
TYPE Bug

According to Pokémon lore, Caterpie is capable of devouring huge leaves bigger than its body size. While Pokémon Go players won't get an opportunity to test its appetite, they can appreciate how this bug-type pokémon can put up a good defense against weaker fighting-, grass- and ground-type pokémon. Curiously, only one of its possible moves is a bug-type attack, so be sure to keep that in mind!

EXPERT ADVICE

Caterpie may be considered a "weak" pokémon, but its small size and propensity to wiggle around the screen can make it a little tricky to catch. You may want to throw a Razz Berry to help calm it down.

#011 METAPOD

CLASSIFICATION Cocoon pokémon
TYPE Bug

In Pokémon lore, Metapod's green shell is similar to an insect's chrysalis but is as hard as steel. Still, while more powerful than Caterpie, this pokémon will have problems against powerful rock-, fire- and flying-type pokémon. After 50 Caterpie candies, Metapod will transform into Butterfree, a powerful flying bug.

EXPERT ADVICE

Metapod shares the same intermediate evolution status with Kakuna, another pupa-like pokémon. Though largely ineffective in a battle, it's worth saving for its final evolution, Butterfree.

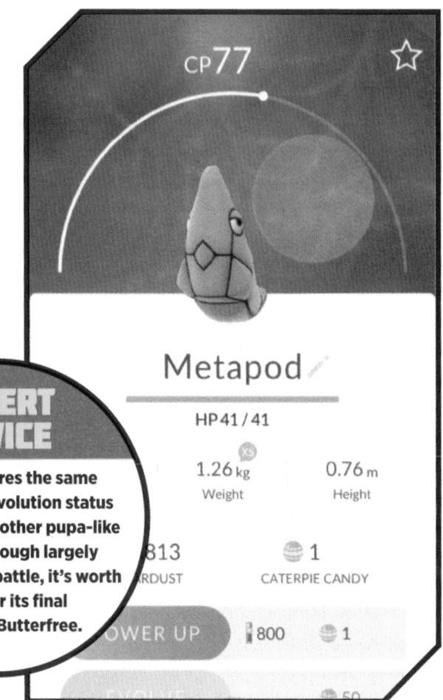

#012 BUTTERFREE

CLASSIFICATION Butterfly pokémon
TYPE Bug/Flying

EXPERT ADVICE

Like other flying pokémon, Butterfree's attacks are most effective against bug, fighting and grass pokémon. Make sure to aim high when trying to capture it with a pokéball in the wild.

Butterfree may not look like the most intimidating pokémon of the 151, but its wings are covered in a poisonous powder that makes it an anxiety-inducing beast in battle. Its compound eyes also allow Butterfree to see better than almost any other pokémon in the game, an advantage it uses to land powerful attacks like Bug Buzz, Psychic, Signal Beam, Bug Bite and Confusion.

#013 WEEDLE

CLASSIFICATION Hairy Bug pokémon
TYPE Bug

Weedle's main defenses come from the poisonous stingers located on its head and tail. Pokémon Go trainers have reported finding it just about anywhere you can think of, including grassy or forested areas. After receiving 12 Weedle candies, it will transform into its next evolutionary phase, Kakuna. Its final form is Beedrill, one of the most fearsome bug-types in the game.

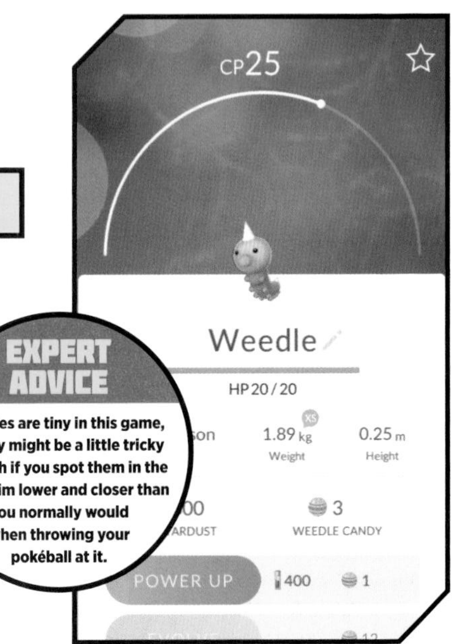

EXPERT ADVICE

Weedles are tiny in this game, so they might be a little tricky to catch if you spot them in the wild. Aim lower and closer than you normally would when throwing your pokéball at it.

#014 KAKUNA

CLASSIFICATION Cocoon pokémon
TYPE Bug/Poison

Kakuna uses its dome-shaped head and back in collaboration with its scythe-like arms to defend itself while in its most delicate cocooned phase. Although it has a variety of possible attack types, this pokémon's main purpose is not to battle but to protect itself until its trainer has collected enough candies to evolve it into Beedrill.

EXPERT ADVICE

Though they may not be powerful in a battle, capturing a lot of Kakunas and its pre-evolved form Weedle can be a quick way to level up. Remember: Every evolution earns you 500 XP.

#015 BEEDRILL

CLASSIFICATION Poison Bee pokémon
TYPE Bug/Poison

Beedrill resembles a massive house wasp that can walk on two legs, has three massive stingers, red eyes and, according to Pokémon lore, packs an even worse temper than its real-world counterparts. Able to learn moves such as Aerial Ace, Sludge Bomb and X-Scissor, Beedrill is not to be trifled with. These pokémon are also more likely to appear fully evolved to higher-level trainers.

EXPERT ADVICE

Beedrill can be evolved directly from Kakuna after giving it 50 Weedle candies. Like other bug-type pokémon, Beedrill's attacks are most effective against grass- and psychic-type pokémon.

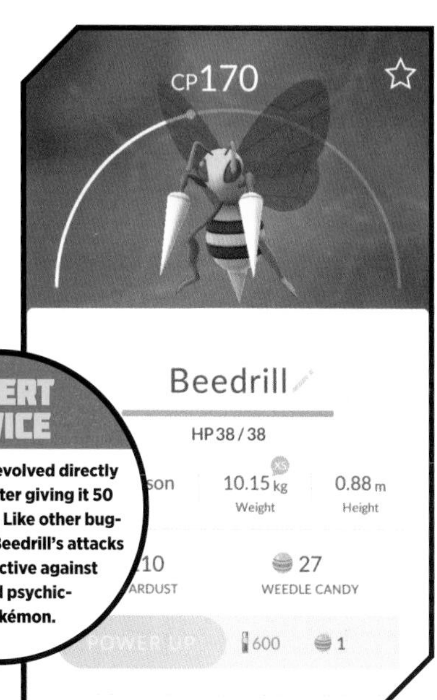

#016 PIDGEY

CLASSIFICATION Tiny Bird pokémon
TYPE Normal/Flying

An extremely sharp honing instinct, strong talons and powerful wings make Pidgey a good hunter, even as a relatively small and unevolved pokémon. Pidgey is also one of the most common monsters you'll find out in the wild. After 12 Pidgey candies, it gains bright red plumage and transforms into the much larger Pidgeotto.

EXPERT ADVICE

Don't pass up this incredibly common pokémon if you see it out in the wild. Lots of players will capture dozens of Pidgeys and evolve them all at once as a strategy to move up levels fast.

#017 PIDGEOTTO

CLASSIFICATION Bird pokémon
TYPE Normal/Flying

Pidgeotto is a much more heavily feathered and fearsome battler than its previous evolutionary stage, Pidgey. At the gym, the much larger bird mainly battles with its massive wings, stocking one of two attacks, including Air Cutter, Twister, Aerial Ace, Steel Wing and Wing Attack. It can be found wherever Pidgeys are also common out in the wild.

EXPERT ADVICE

Once you fully evolve one Pidgey, it seems like this intermediary evolution becomes far more common out in the wild. Catch it, save up Pidgey candy and evolve for a quick XP boost.

#018 PIDGEOT

CLASSIFICATION Bird pokémon
TYPE Normal/Flying

After receiving 50 more Pidgey candies, the fearsome Pidgeotto swaps out its red plumage for yellow forehead feathers and reaches its ultimate form: Pidgeot. In pokémon lore, it's rumored that this pokémon can fly faster than the speed of sound, aiding it in flying attacks like Hurricane and Air Cutter.

EXPERT ADVICE

Due to the overwhelming abundance of Pidgeys in Pokémon Go, this will likely be one of the first pokémon you fully evolve. As a flying type, it is weak against electric, ice and rock pokémon.

#019 RATTATA

CLASSIFICATION Mouse pokémon
TYPE Normal

Like its real-world counterparts, Rattata is a highly adaptative pokémon that can live anywhere food (or garbage) is plentiful. Seek them out day or night in a wide variety of cities, suburbs and rural areas. After receiving 50 Rattata candies, this small mouse pokémon will grow into the much larger, stronger Raticate.

EXPERT ADVICE

Capturing every single Rattata you see in the wild can be annoying, but you can evolve multiple as a strategy to level-up quickly. Use a lucky egg while you're evolving to double your progress.

#020 RATICATE

CLASSIFICATION Mouse pokémon
TYPE Normal

The first thing you'll notice about Raticate is its enormous incisors, which never stop growing and give it a powerful bite in the midst of a battle. Its signature shriek is much lower and louder than its pre-evolved form, Rattata, and sends many enemies running the other way. Just don't depend on it to dominate rock- or steel-type pokémon.

EXPERT ADVICE

If you live in a city, Raticate will most likely be one of your first evolutions in the game. Its battle attacks can include Bite, Quick Attack, Dig, Hyper Beam and Hyper Fang.

#021 SPEAROW

CLASSIFICATION Tiny Bird pokémon
TYPE Normal/Flying

Don't mistake Spearow for its softer-plumed relative, Pidgey. In Pokémon lore, this bird-like pokémon is notoriously bad tempered, making it quick to use its sharp beak and talons. As befits its aerial nature, Spearow can learn Twister, a dragon-type attack. After 50 Spearow candies, it will evolve into Fearow.

EXPERT ADVICE

Like Pidgey, Spearow is a bird-like creature that is likely to be incredibly common while you're out hunting for pokémon. Catch a lot and evolve them all at once for a quick XP boost in the game.

#022 FEAROW

CLASSIFICATION Beak pokémon
TYPE Normal/Flying

In the Pokémon world, Fearow uses its massive wingspan to maintain the stamina to fly for an entire day without rest. In Pokémon Go, this bird pokémon can lay the smack down on fighting-type pokémon with flying-type attacks. This pokémon can also pack flying-, steel-, ground- and dragon-type attacks.

EXPERT ADVICE

Don't confuse Fearow's silhouette in your pokédex for a legendary bird! The evolved form of Spearow is likely to become one of the most common big birds in the game.

#023 EKANS

CLASSIFICATION Snake pokémon
TYPE Poison

Although Ekans might look like your average garden snake, albeit purple, don't discount this poison-type pokémon. Apart from its poison-type special moves, Ekans can use a normal move—Wrap—to coil itself around its enemies. After 50 Ekans candies, it evolves into the fearsome cobra-like Arbok.

EXPERT ADVICE

Like many poison pokémon, Ekans's attacks are super effective against fairy- and grass-type pokémon. They are also fast jumpers, so watch your pokéballs when trying to capture it.

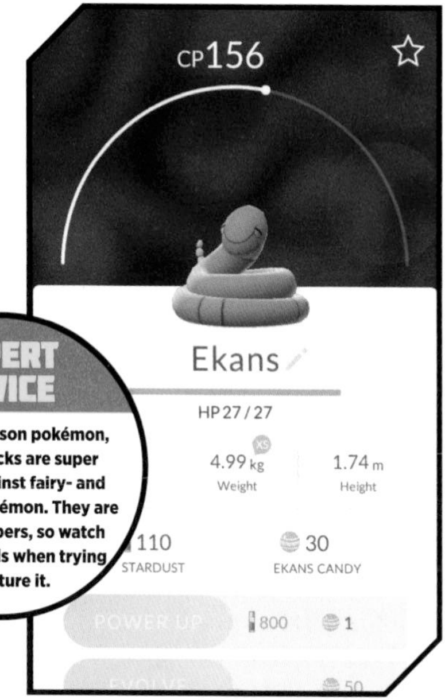

#024 ARBOK

CLASSIFICATION Cobra pokémon
TYPE Poison

With the power to constrict and even flatten a steel oil drum, Arbok is good to have in a Pokémon Go trainer's arsenal. No trainer's pokémon will want to get stuck in this poison cobra's coils. In addition to its poison-type moves, Arbok can also have two dark-type moves, Bite and Dark pulse. Dark-type moves are particularly potent against fairy-type pokémon, such as Clefairy.

EXPERT ADVICE

Like other poison-type pokémon, Arbok is most effective against grass-type pokémon, but it does not fare well against rock- or other poison-type pokémon in a battle.

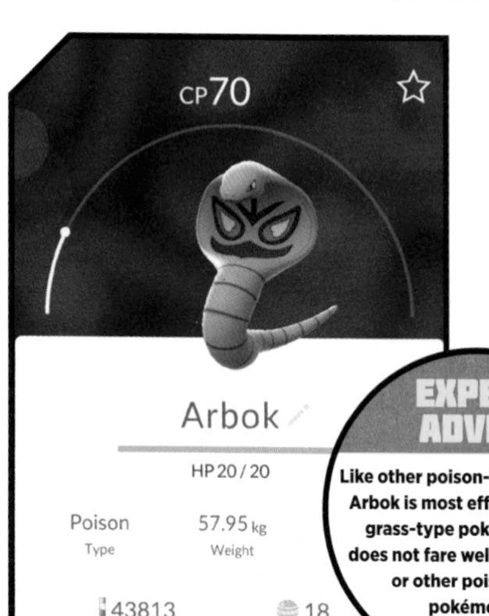

#025 PIKACHU

CLASSIFICATION Mouse pokémon
TYPE Electric

Pikachu is undoubtedly the most recognizable of the 151 original pokémon, serving as the franchise mascot and one of the main stars of the original anime series. In pokémon lore, Pikachu stores energy in its red cheek glands until it is ready to unleash an attack, and it uses its tail as a grounding agent to keep itself safe from all that electricity.

EXPERT ADVICE

To get Pikachu as your starter pokémon from Professor Willow, continually run away from Bulbasaur, Squirtle or Charmander on your initial capture. It will eventually appear on your map.

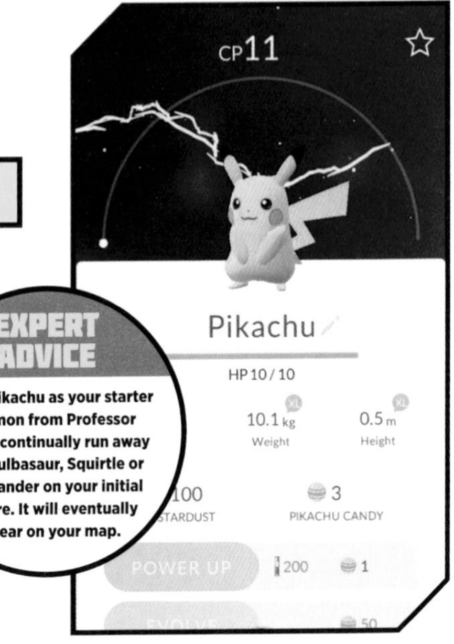

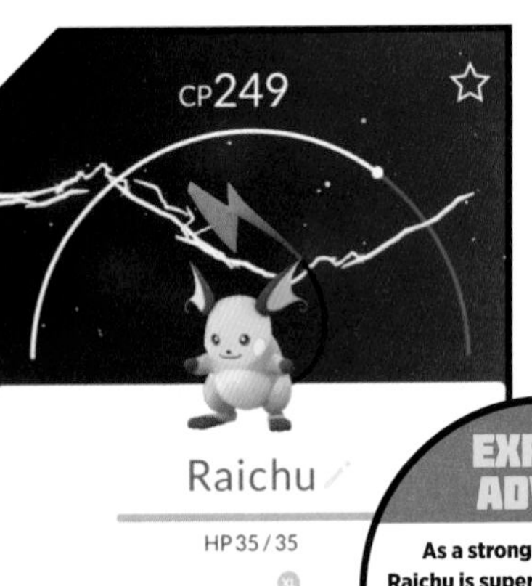

#026 RAICHU

CLASSIFICATION Mouse pokémon
TYPE Electric

If you work hard enough to save up 50 Pikachu candies (a difficult feat, as the mouse pokémon is a relatively rare capture in the game), you can evolve it into Raichu, which is able to store far more energy and powerful attacks in its body than its pre-evolved counterpart. As with Pikachu, search for Raichu near forests and other wooded areas.

EXPERT ADVICE

As a strong electric-type, Raichu is super effective against flying- and water-type pokémon in a gym battle. However, ground types can easily absorb its lighting-bolt attacks.

#027 SANDSHREW

CLASSIFICATION Mouse pokémon
TYPE Ground

Sandshrews use their tawny, brick-patterned skin to help them blend in with cliffsides, rocks and of course, sand. This little mouse can pack normal-, ground-, rock- and electric-type attacks in its battle roster. After 50 Sandshrew candies, Sandshrew will grow spikes on its back and hands, tranforming into the formidable Sandslash.

EXPERT ADVICE

Player reports suggest searching for Sandshrew in places with dry, arid climates or at the beach. That being said, I've seen him in a number of public parks, so keep an eye out everywhere.

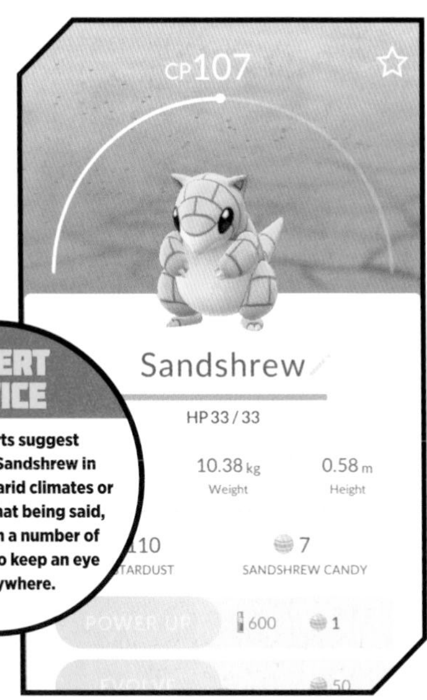

#028 SANDSLASH

CLASSIFICATION Mouse pokémon
TYPE Ground

This pokémon may technically be included in the mouse category, but if those big brown spikes and rolling attacks are any sign, Sandslash is definitely an homage to real-world hedgehogs and armadillos. Just like its former evolutionary phase, this pokémon prefers desert environments, where it can easily burrow down into the sand.

EXPERT ADVICE

Sandslash is a far rarer find than its pre-evolved form, Sandshrew. It seems to escape from pokéballs pretty easily, so make sure you have a solid stash in your backpack if you want to catch one.

#029 NIDORAN♀

CLASSIFICATION Poison Pin pokémon
TYPE Poison

Though this short, blue, rabbit-like pokemon is cute, it has a poison-tipped spike on its forehead that can dole out serious damage in an attack. The female Nidoran may also pack dark- and normal-type attacks. After receiving 25 Nidoran candies, this pokémon will evolve into its intermediary phase, Nidorina.

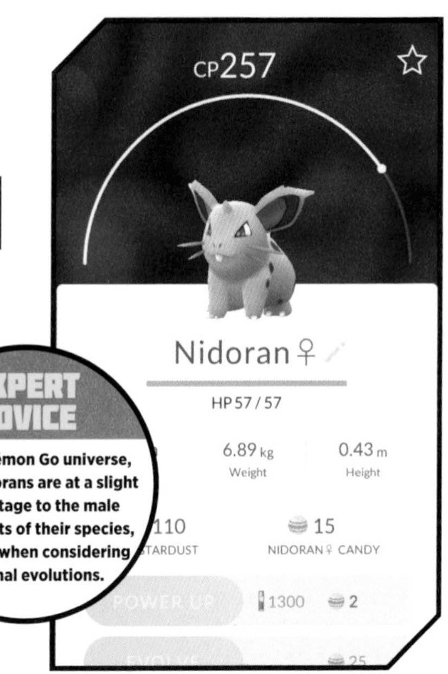

EXPERT ADVICE

In the Pokémon Go universe, female Nidorans are at a slight disadvantage to the male counterparts of their species, especially when considering their final evolutions.

#030 NIDORINA

CLASSIFICATION Poison Pin pokémon
TYPE Poison

In a gym battle, Nidorina will often turn to its sharp teeth and claws to defend itself from harm. However, some subsets of the species are also able to emit a poisonous secretion from their bodies, which they can use in a special Sludge Bomb attack. After 100 Nidoran candies, Nidorina will evolve into the powerful Nidoqueen, its final form.

EXPERT ADVICE

As a poison-type pokémon, Nidorina is most effective against fairy- and grass-type pokémon in a battle. Be careful using it against ground-, psychic- or ghost-type pokémon.

#031 NIDOQUEEN

CLASSIFICATION Drill pokémon
TYPE Poison/Ground

Though it follows a similar evolutionary path to its male counterpart, Nidoking, the female Nidoqueen is equipped for different attacks. This species is often able to use its massive size in the game to tackle and incapacitate any opponent, or to create strong tremors by stomping its feet in the grass.

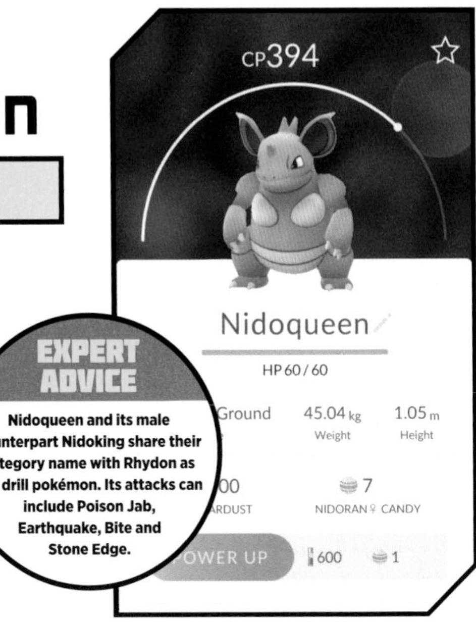

EXPERT ADVICE

Nidoqueen and its male counterpart Nidoking share their category name with Rhydon as the drill pokémon. Its attacks can include Poison Jab, Earthquake, Bite and Stone Edge.

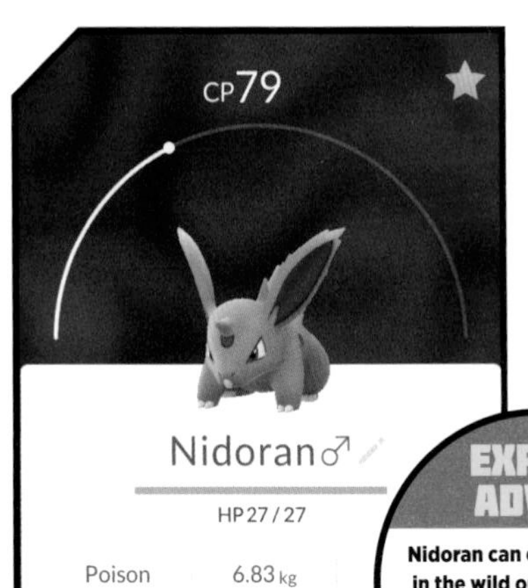

#032 NIDORAN♂

CLASSIFICATION Poison Pin pokémon
TYPE Poison

The purple, male version of Nidoran uses its enormous ears to listen for the sound of approaching enemies, according to lore. Its poison moves, such as Poison Sting, make it a good counter for fairy-type pokémon. After receiving 25 male Nidoran candies, it will evolve into its next evolutionary phase, Nidorino.

EXPERT ADVICE

Nidoran can either be found in the wild or hatched from a 5km egg. It seems to be fairly common in suburban areas or near giant fields.

#033 NIDORINO

CLASSIFICATION Poison Pin pokémon
TYPE Poison

As soon as it evolves from the male Nidoran, it's rumored that Nidorino's poison horn becomes as hard as a diamond, making it a much more formidable opponent in gym battles. Like the rest of its kind, Nidorino can be most commonly found in hot grasslands and plains. After 100 Nidoran candies, this pokémon will evolve into Nidoking.

EXPERT ADVICE

In a battle, Nidorino's quick attacks can include Peck, Poison Jab and Poison Sting. Special attacks, or "charge moves" can include Horn Attack, Dig and Sludge Bomb.

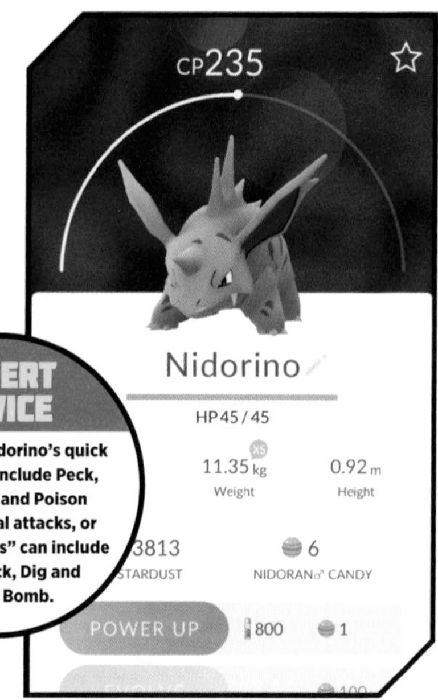

#034 NIDOKING

CLASSIFICATION Drill pokémon
TYPE Poison/Ground

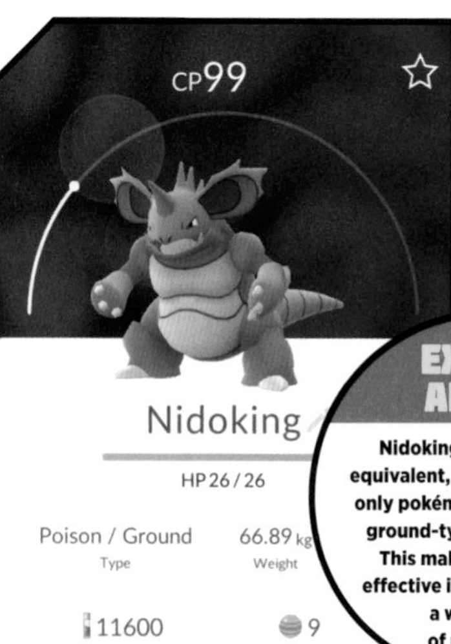

EXPERT ADVICE

Nidoking and its female equivalent, Nidoqueen are the only pokémon with a poison/ground-type combination. This makes them highly effective in a battle against a wide array of pokémon.

Though its prior evolutions resemble cute, poisonous rabbits, a fully formed Nidoking is more akin in its appearance to an evil purple unicorn. This pokémon can pack a number of powerful battle moves, including Megahorn, Sludge Wave, Poison Jab and Fury Cutter. Like its feminine counterpart, Nidoqueen, Nidoking may also stock a powerful Earthquake attack.

#035 CLEFAIRY

CLASSIFICATION Fairy pokémon
TYPE Fairy

In Pokémon lore, Clefairy is best known to congregate in dark, high-altitude regions that remind it of its ancestral home, Mt. Moon. The cute pink puff of a pokémon may stock normal-, psychic- or fairy-type attacks. After receiving 50 Clefairy candies, it will grow wings and evolve into Clefable, one of the rarest monsters in the Pokémon Go universe.

EXPERT ADVICE

Like other pink fairy pokémon, Clefairy's attacks are most effective against dragon- and fighting-type pokémon. Search for it at night, basking under the light of the moon.

#036 CLEFABLE

CLASSIFICATION Fairy pokémon
TYPE Fairy

Clefable is so spooked by the presence of human beings that it is almost never seen in the wild (which is why Pokémon Go trainers rarely find them). Its dazzling Gleam attack has been known to incapacitate even the strongest opponent in a battle. However, according to Pokémon lore, Clefable prefers to use its fairy powers for protection, rather than conflict. This monster may also stock a few powerful psychic-type attacks.

EXPERT ADVICE

Clefable evolves from Clefairy after collecting 50 Clefairy candies. It is known to take strolls near lakes on quiet, moonlit nights, but don't worry about having to take a swim to catch one.

#037 VULPIX

CLASSIFICATION Fox pokémon
TYPE Fire

Lore states that every brown and orange Vulpix has flames inside of its body, which never go out and are used to fuel its wide array of fire-type attacks. This pokémon also has six tails, which it may use for balance during Quick Attack or Body Slam moves. After receiving 50 candies, Vulpix will sprout three more tails and evolve into the graceful, ethereal Ninetales.

EXPERT ADVICE

Vulpix can be hatched from a 5km egg. It can also be found in the wild but is a relatively rare find so far. Try searching for it in grassy or forested areas.

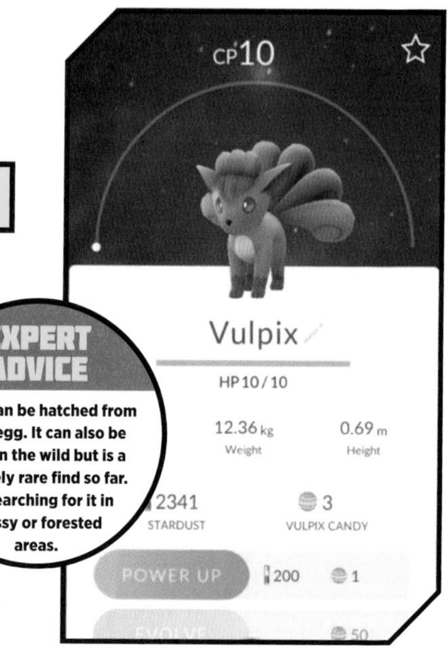

#038 NINETALES

CLASSIFICATION Fox pokémon
TYPE Fire

Along with its powerful fire attacks, Ninetales is known for its penchant to curse enemy pokémon with powerful black magic in the midst of a gym battle. One of its main moves, Feint Attack, is one of the few dark-type moves included in the game, giving a certain subset of the species a big advantage against both fairy- and water-type pokémon.

EXPERT ADVICE

Ninetales is a favorite among trainers for a reason. Not only is it beautiful, its strong fire attacks are incredibly effective against bug, grass, ice and steel pokémon in battle.

#039 JIGGLYPUFF

CLASSIFICATION Balloon pokémon
TYPE Normal/Fairy

Jigglypuff may look harmless, but this big ball of air is actually a solid fairy-type fighter in battle. Its song is known throughout the Pokémon world as either a soothing lullabye or a catchy, hypnotizing nuisance. Search for it in lush fields and grassy meadows, where it's easiest for this pokémon to breathe.

EXPERT ADVICE

Jigglypuff can be captured in the wild or by hatching it from a 5km egg. According to its IV stats, Jigglypuff has one of the highest staminas of a pre-evolved pokémon in the game.

#040 WIGGLYTUFF

CLASSIFICATION Balloon pokémon
TYPE Fairy

After receiving 50 Jigglypuff candies, the longer-eared Wigglytuff will emerge from its evolutionary ether. In the midst of a fight, Wigglytuff may use a Dazzling Gleam ability to make the pokémon they are battling become infatuated with them, weakening their blows. However, some Wigglytuffs prefer to Play Rough, using a more full-frontal attack.

EXPERT ADVICE

Wigglytuff is worth saving candies for. It's highly effective against dragon and fighting types, plus, only poison and steel types are super effective against it, the latter of which is pretty rare.

#041 ZUBAT

CLASSIFICATION Bat pokémon
TYPE Poison

In Pokémon lore, the sun is said to burn a Zubat's body, so search for this pokémon at night, or in shady areas like forests and indoor enclosures, where it is more likely to dwell. Zubats don't have eyes, so they use echolocation to aid in attacks like Poison Fang, Air Cutter and Sludge Bomb, which are by far their most common battle moves.

EXPERT ADVICE

While incredibly common, Zubats are one of the most frustrating pokémon to catch. Make sure to aim your throws higher and farther than usual when attempting to capture one.

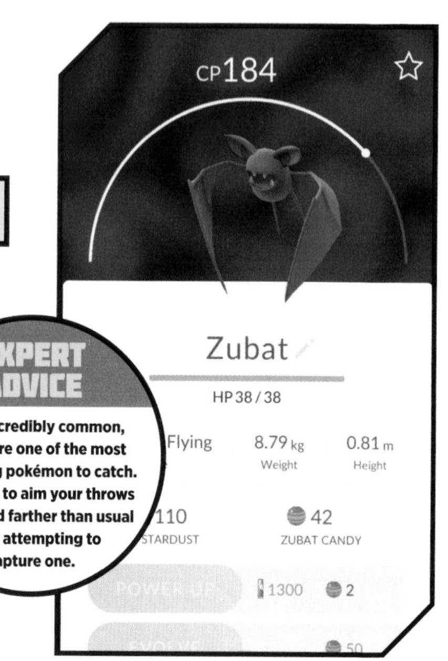

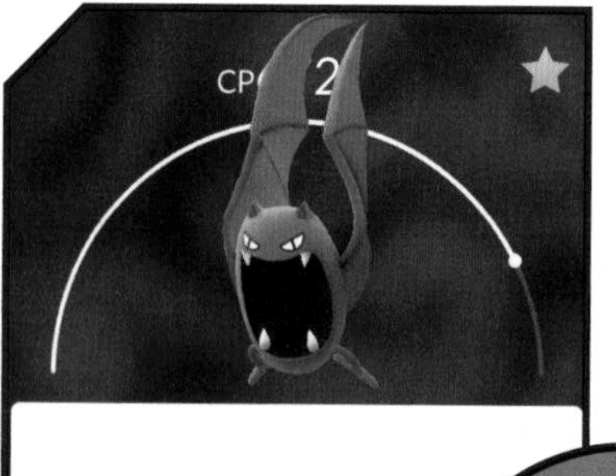

#042 GOLBAT

CLASSIFICATION Bat pokémon
TYPE Poison/Flying

After 50 Zubat candies, the tiny bat pokémon transforms into Golbat, a massive flying beast with four deadly fangs. Though it loves to bite, Golbat's most powerful possible move is Wing Attack. Search for this poisonous, blood-sucking beast at night or on the shady side of skyscrapers. It seems to enjoy urban, Gothic landscapes as its primary home.

EXPERT ADVICE

In fights, Golbat holds a big advantage over ground, psychic, electric and rock pokémon. Like Zubat, It's incredibly frustrating to catch in the wild.

#043 ODDISH

CLASSIFICATION Weed pokémon
TYPE Grass/Poison

Oddish is a typically nocturnal plant creature that wanders in the darkness to spread its seeds across forests, grasslands and cityscapes. Its grass-type attacks are useful against the water-type pokémon typically found in gyms. After receiving 25 Oddish candies, this bulb-like creature will start to flower, evolving into a drooling Gloom.

EXPERT ADVICE

Oddish can actually be found day or night and is a relatively common find in the Pokémon Go universe. Its attacks can include Acid, Absorb, Giga Drain, Mega Drain, Sludge Bomb and Moonblast.

#044 GLOOM

CLASSIFICATION Weed pokémon
TYPE Grass/Poison

Don't make fun of Gloom's perpetual drooling expression. The liquid hanging from its mouth is rumored in Pokémon lore to be a valuable nectar that can be used to either attract other pokémon or defend itself during an attack. Perhaps that's where one of its quick moves, Acid, comes from. This pokémon may also stock a Razor Leaf, Moonblast, Petal Blizzard or Sludge Bomb attack in its battle roster.

EXPERT ADVICE

Gloom looks pretty cool, but after catching and trading for 100 more Oddish candies, you can evolve Gloom into Vileplume, a much larger and more powerful flower pokémon.

#045 VILEPLUME

CLASSIFICATION Flower pokémon
TYPE Grass/Poison

After receiving 100 Oddish candies, Gloom will transform into Vileplume, a larger, but much cuter flower pokémon. But don't be fooled by its calming pink and blue appearance. According to Pokémon lore, Vileplume's bloom releases a pollen that is thought to be allergenic to humans and pokémon alike. Search for it in grassy areas.

EXPERT ADVICE

Despite being a grass/poison-type pokémon, Vileplume may be packing Moonblast, a super powerful fairy attack. If you snag one of these rare subsets, make sure to try it out against a dragon type.

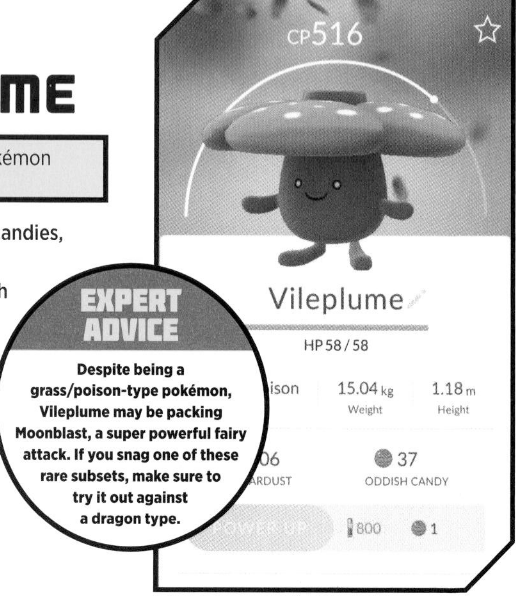

#046 PARAS

CLASSIFICATION Mushroom pokémon
TYPE Bug/Grass

EXPERT ADVICE

Search for this bug-type pokémon in grassy areas like parks, fields or wooded areas. If you're having a hard time finding it, walk. Paras can also be hatched from a 5km egg.

Paras is a cicada-like pokémon that is covered in red and yellow mushrooms known in Japanese as tochukaso, which grow from spores on its body and are rumored to have been growing there since birth. It takes 50 Paras candies to evolve this creature into Parasect, a monstrous insect with a much larger, more powerful mushroom colony on its back.

#047 PARASECT

CLASSIFICATION Mushroom pokémon
TYPE Bug/Grass

According to Pokémon lore, when Paras evolves into Parasect, the powerful poison mushrooms on its body coalesce into a single colony, which take full control of its brain. Perhaps that's where this insect's super-powerful Solar Beam attack comes from. Paras may also stock an X-Scissor or Cross Poison special move, which are faster and more efficient than the former attack.

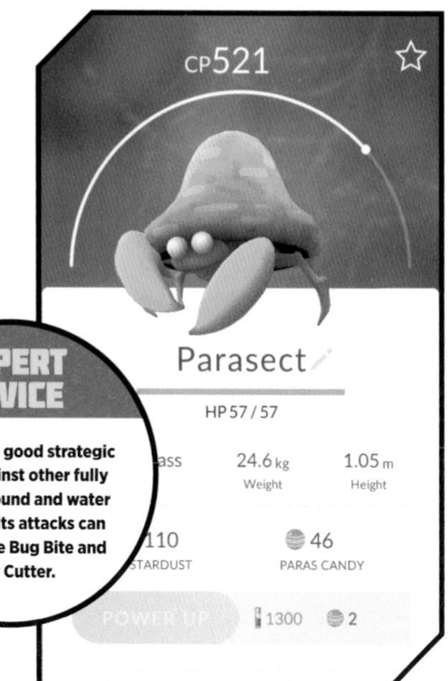

EXPERT ADVICE

Parasect is a good strategic battler against other fully evolved ground and water pokémon. Its attacks can also include Bug Bite and Fury Cutter.

#048 VENONAT

CLASSIFICATION Insect pokémon
TYPE Bug/Poison

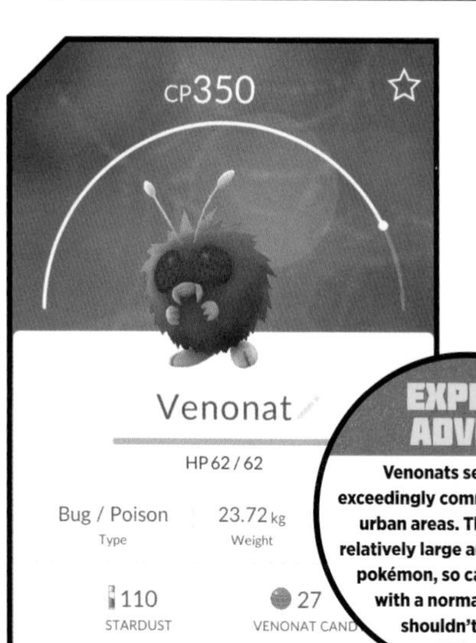

Venonat's huge red eyes can shoot lasers, aiding in its possible Psybeam and Signal Beam special charge attacks. Its white antenna, purple fur and fangs are also oozing with venom, which help contribute to some additional bug and poison-type battle moves. Venonat will grow wings and evolve into Venomoth after receiving 50 Venonat candies.

EXPERT ADVICE

Venonats seem to be exceedingly common at night in urban areas. They're also a relatively large and non-fleeing pokémon, so capturing one with a normal pokéball shouldn't be too difficult.

#049 VENOMOTH

CLASSIFICATION Poison Moth pokémon
TYPE Bug/Poison

Once evolved, Venonat becomes the winged purple pokémon known as Venomoth. Able to attack with the likes of its powerful Poison Fang move, Venomoth can also be very useful for its quick Confusion fast attack and its paralyzing Psychic special move. Because of its versatility, this pokémon can be a game-changer in difficult battles.

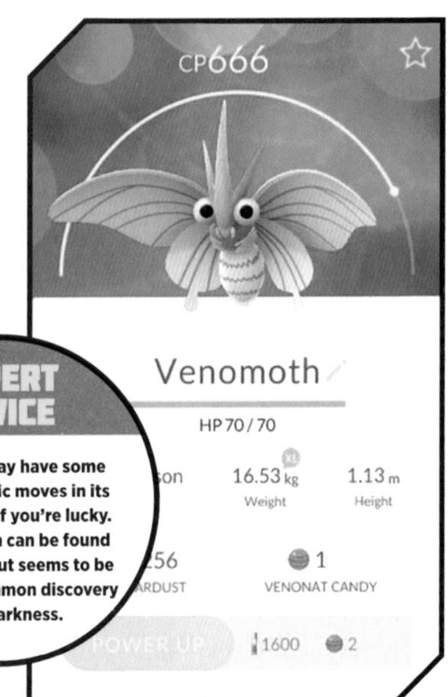

EXPERT ADVICE

Venomoth may have some hidden psychic moves in its attack roster if you're lucky. This pokémon can be found day or night but seems to be a far more common discovery in the darkness.

#050 DIGLETT

CLASSIFICATION Mole pokémon
TYPE Ground

EXPERT ADVICE

Search for Digletts in the countryside or other places where fields and dirt are plentiful. Diglett can also be hatched from a 5km egg.

With its head perpetually periscoped out of the ground it burrows in, Diglett could very well be one of the largest pokémon in the world beneath the surface. When used in a battle, it can distract and damage other pokémon using fast-acting ground tactics such as Mud Shot and Mud Bomb, or its most powerful charge move, Dig. After 50 Diglett candies, it evolves into Dugtrio.

#051 DUGTRIO

CLASSIFICATION Mole pokémon
TYPE Ground

The evolved form of Diglett, Dugtrio is actually comprised of Diglett triplets sharing the same body, thoughts and functions. Players can make use of this pokémon's relatively quick attack speed, calling upon fast moves such as Sucker Punch and Mud Shot that are sure to catch an opponent off guard. Dugtrio can also be quite powerful when its Earthquake charge move is used.

EXPERT ADVICE

Dugtrio has one of the highest base speeds of all the ground-type pokémon, so be sure to throw your pokéball quickly before it burrows back down into the ground to escape capture.

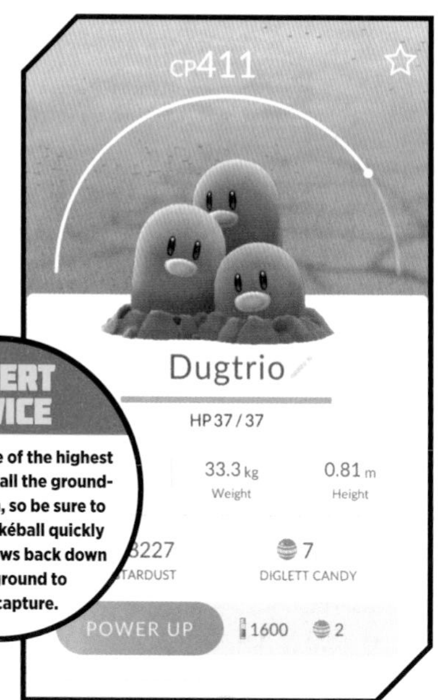

#052 MEOWTH

CLASSIFICATION Scratch Cat pokémon
TYPE Normal

According to lore, the Scratch Cat pokémon known as Meowth is extremely attracted to shiny objects. Cat-like fast moves like Bite and Scratch make Meowth a nuissance to other pokémon in battle, but it can also do more devastating damage with special attacks that include Dark Pulse and Night Slash, which can be critical if timed well.

EXPERT ADVICE

Heads up using Meowth in a battle: The attacks of normal-type pokémon are not super effective against any other type of pokémon. Match it up according to CP, not special abilities.

#053 PERSIAN

CLASSIFICATION Classy Cat pokémon
TYPE Normal

A Meowth able to find 50 of its candies can evolve into Persian, a pokémon believed to be so aggressive, it will even scratch its own trainer. For fast attacks, Persian can use Feint Attack, which involves approaching the opponent before hitting them with a Sucker Punch. For a powerful charge move, Persian can use the powerful Fairy move, Play Rough.

EXPERT ADVICE

Use Persian against ghost pokémon like Gengar, Haunter and Gastly in a gym battle. In my experience, its attacks have been highly effective against them.

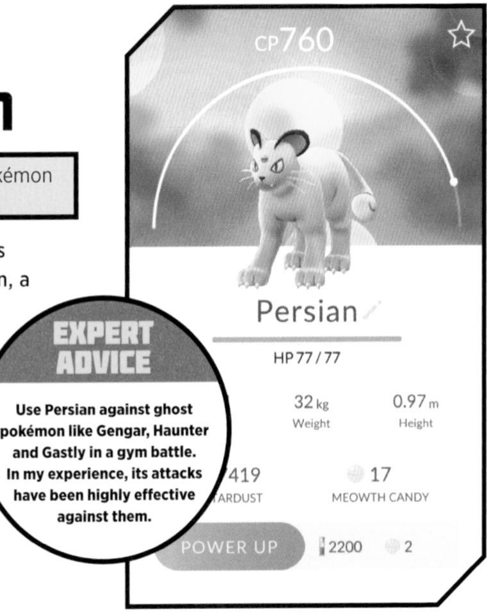

#054 PSYDUCK

CLASSIFICATION Duck pokémon
TYPE Psychic

According to pokémon lore, Psyduck is armed with a mysterious power that involves the generation of powerful brain waves. When a player chooses Psyduck for a gym battle, they may see success when using its Psychic moves, Psybeam and Zen Headbutt. Psyduck can also attack with more traditional tactics, such as its charge move, Cross Chop.

EXPERT ADVICE

Psyduck may not be highly effective in a battle, but its evolved state Golduck can be a game-changer at the gym. This pokémon is definitely worth saving and exchanging for candies.

#055 GOLDUCK

CLASSIFICATION Duck pokémon
TYPE Water

After 50 candies, Psyduck will become Golduck, a bipedal creature with webbed feet that give it the ability to swim at incredibly fast speeds. When using that speed in a battle, Golduck can utilize the likes of Confusion and Water Gun. Its most devastating special attack, Hydro Pump, is particularly effective against fire, rock and ground types of pokémon.

EXPERT ADVICE

Long-time players know Golduck is one of the few pokémon obtainable in every core series game. In Pokémon Go, its special attacks can also include Aqua Jet, Psychic and Ice Beam.

#056 MANKEY

CLASSIFICATION Pig Monkey pokémon
TYPE Fighting

A shaggy pokémon resembling a monkey with the snout of a pig, Mankey is known to be a fierce fighter with a short temper. Using this pig monkey pokémon's physical fighting skills can serve a player well in battle, with Mankey's Karate Chop, Low Sweep and Brick Break all serving as effective moves for overwhelming opponents.

EXPERT ADVICE

Mankey is the shortest fighting-type pokémon, so aim low when you attempt to capture it in the wild. That being said, they also jump a lot, making them even more difficult to catch.

#057 PRIMEAPE

CLASSIFICATION Pig Monkey pokémon
TYPE Fighting

The even angrier second stage of Mankey, Primeape will completely lose its temper if a creature even decides to make eye contact with it. Like its earlier stage, Primeape's anger can be used to a player's advantage in battle with a variety of Fighting moves such as Low Kick and Cross Chop, and it can even charge with one dark move, Night Slash.

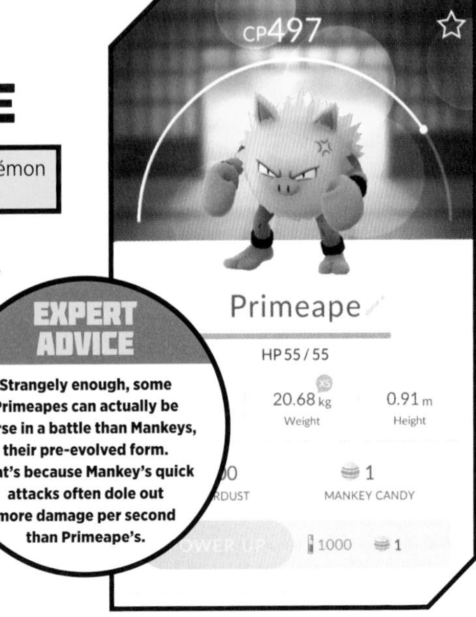

EXPERT ADVICE

Strangely enough, some Primeapes can actually be worse in a battle than Mankeys, their pre-evolved form. That's because Mankey's quick attacks often dole out more damage per second than Primeape's.

#058 GROWLITHE

CLASSIFICATION Puppy pokémon
TYPE Fire

Known to be exceptionally loyal and a fearless defender of its trainer, Growlithe lives up to what one would expect of a puppy pokémon. Even when battling more skilled and stronger pokémon, Growlithe can be formidable with its Bite move or its quick-hitting Ember. For battles that require bigger moves, Growlithe can pull out its Body Slam and Flamethrower.

EXPERT ADVICE

According to player reports, Growlithes are incredibly common in dry, arid regions like California, Arizona and Nevada. However, in forests or grassy regions, they are quite rare to capture.

#059 ARCANINE

CLASSIFICATION Canine pokémon
TYPE Fire

After 50 candies, Growlithe becomes Arcanine, the noble yet dangerous canine fire pokémon with black stripes resembling those of a tiger. Lore states Arcanine is incredibly speedy, capable of running 6,200 miles in a single day, making it a particularly impressive catch that any player should be proud to show off in a gym battle.

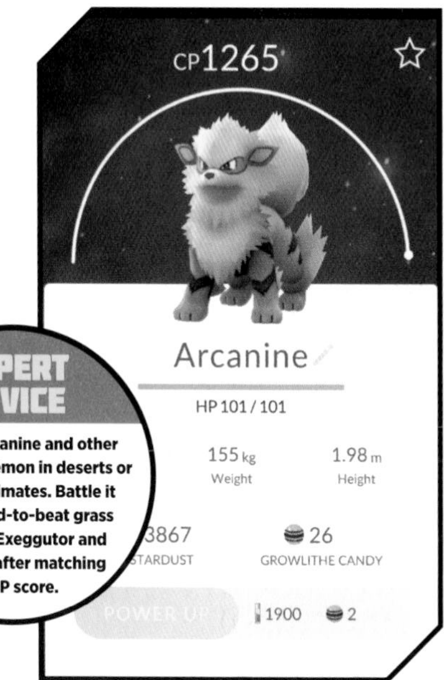

EXPERT ADVICE

Look for Arcanine and other fire-type pokémon in deserts or other dry climates. Battle it against hard-to-beat grass types like Exeggutor and Venusaur after matching by CP score.

#060 POLIWAG

CLASSIFICATION Tadpole pokémon
TYPE Water

Often found near freshwater, Poliwags are known for their signature thin skin. This water pokémon's skin is also quite flexible, making it useful in battles against pokémon that rely on Bite moves or fang-based attacks. Poliwag can display a fairly diverse array of moves, including Body Slam, Bubble Beam and Mud Bomb.

EXPERT ADVICE

Poliwag is relatively common in regions with water nearby. To get a pokémon of this species with higher CP to either evolve or take into battle, try hatching it from a 5km egg.

#061 POLIWHIRL

CLASSIFICATION Tadpole pokémon
TYPE Water

After 25 candies, Poliwag becomes much more useful on land as it grows limbs and becomes Poliwhirl. In its evolved state, this pokémon is a reliable choice for any gym battle, fending off opponents with attacks such as Mud Shot. But as capable as this pokémon is, it still pales in comparison to its ultimate evolved form, Poliwrath.

EXPERT ADVICE

Poliwhirl can also have a combination of both water and ground attacks in its battle arsenal, including Bubble, Bubble Beam, Mud Bomb and Scald.

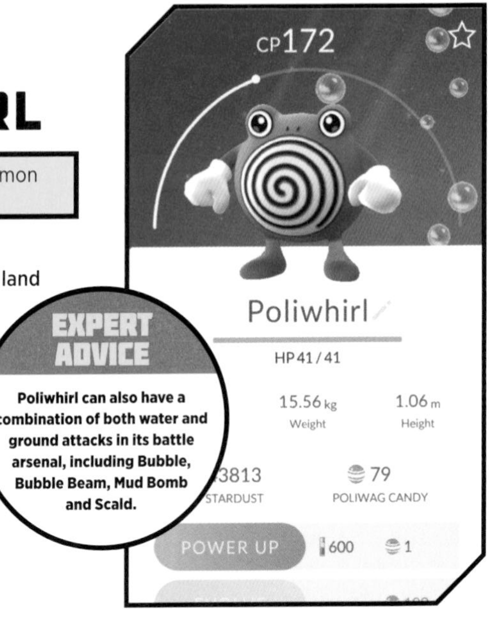

#062 POLIWRATH

CLASSIFICATION Tadpole pokémon
TYPE Water/Fighting

The ultimate stage of Poliwag, the intimidating tadpole pokémon known as Poliwrath packs a new punch with its muscles, which never fatigue, and its newfound fighting ability. Poliwrath can overpower other pokémon by blasting them with Hydro Pump, nailing them with an Ice Punch or grabbing them in Submission.

EXPERT ADVICE

Poliwrath is great in a battle against fire, ground, normal and rock types. its also one of the strongest pokémon you can get as a low-level player, so save up those Poliwag candies.

#063 ABRA

CLASSIFICATION Psi pokémon
TYPE Psychic

Even though it sleeps for 18 hours a day, Abra remains aware of any incoming danger around it and can therefore respond accordingly. Its Psychic moves, Zen Headbutt and Psyshock, can be very effective against poison and fighting types of pokémon. Abra can even pull off Signal Beam, a bug-type move, as a special attack. It evolves into Kadabra after gathering 25 Abra candies.

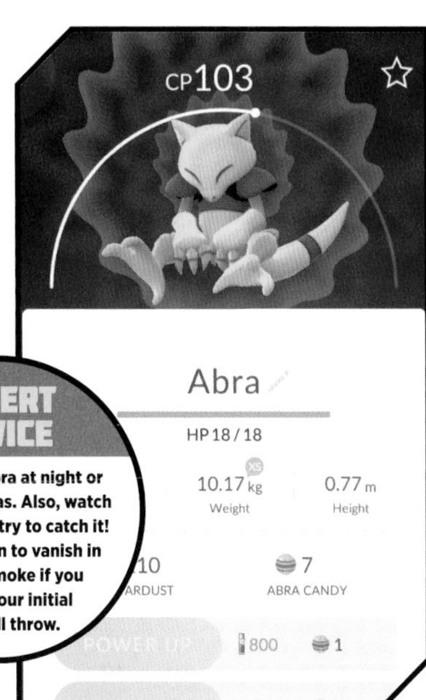

EXPERT ADVICE

Search for Abra at night or by coastal areas. Also, watch out when you try to catch it! Abra is known to vanish in a puff of smoke if you miss on your initial pokéball throw.

#064 KADABRA

CLASSIFICATION Psi pokémon
TYPE Psychic

Once Abra evolves into Kadabra, it becomes a bit harder to handle, as many feel it can only be trained by those with a strong psyche. With an arsenal comprised of psychic, fairy and ghost moves, Kadabra can outmaneuver opponents with the likes of Psycho Cut, Dazzling Beam and Shadow Ball, particularly if it's battling fighting or poison types of pokémon.

EXPERT ADVICE

If you want to defeat a fellow trainer's Kadabra at the gym, try using a powerful insect pokémon like Parasect, Butterfree or Paras, which are highly effective against psychic types.

#065 ALAKAZAM

CLASSIFICATION Psi pokémon
TYPE Psychic

Alakazam, the final evolution of Abra, is considered to be one of the most powerful psi pokémon. For quick, effective hits in a gym batle, players can use Alakazam's Confusion and Psycho Cut moves to disorient and take down the competition. To do the most damage, though, the player can use Alakazam's Psychic move to hit the opposing pokémon with a strong telekinetic force.

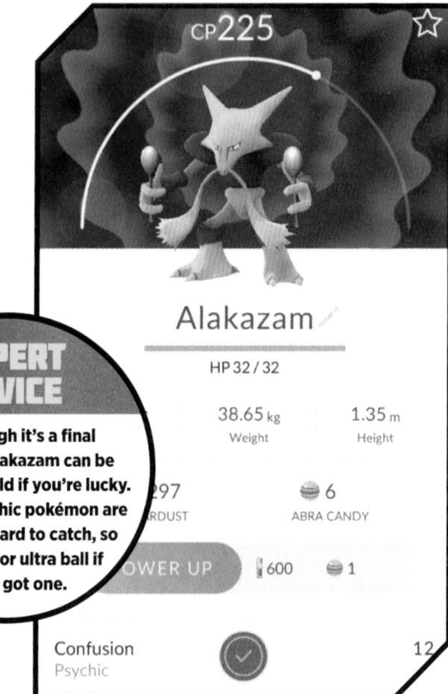

EXPERT ADVICE

Even though it's a final evolution, Alakazam can be found in the wild if you're lucky. However, psychic pokémon are notoriously hard to catch, so use a great or ultra ball if you've got one.

#066 MACHOP

CLASSIFICATION Superpower pokémon
TYPE Fighting

Covered with muscles that never shrink weaken or soften no matter how much they're used, Machop is the perfect example of a small pokémon with exceptional strength. Pokémon lore suggests this little monster could hurl 100 adult humans! But when battling fellow pokémon, Machop uses its fighting-style fast moves Low Kick and Karate Chop and charge moves like Brick Break.

EXPERT ADVICE

Machops are known to punch pokéballs away when you try to capture them in the wild, so make sure to aim carefully.

#067 MACHOKE

CLASSIFICATION Superpower pokémon
TYPE Fighting

When a Machop is able to collect 25 candies, it evolves into Machoke, a muscle-bound and battle-ready pokémon. For players who are going up against dark, ice, rock or steel pokémon in a battle, Machoke can be a very effective choice. Its fast moves Karate Chop and Low Kick can catch opponents off guard, while its Cross Chop special attack can do major damage.

EXPERT ADVICE

Fighting-type pokémon like Machoke love competition, so keep an eye out for them around sports centers and stadiums. They also may congregate around larger pokémon gyms.

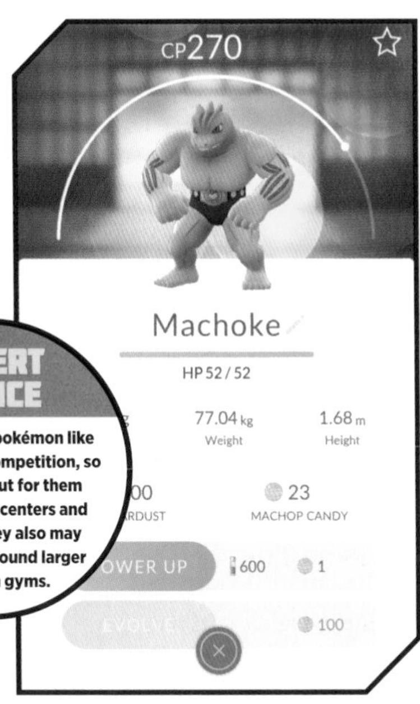

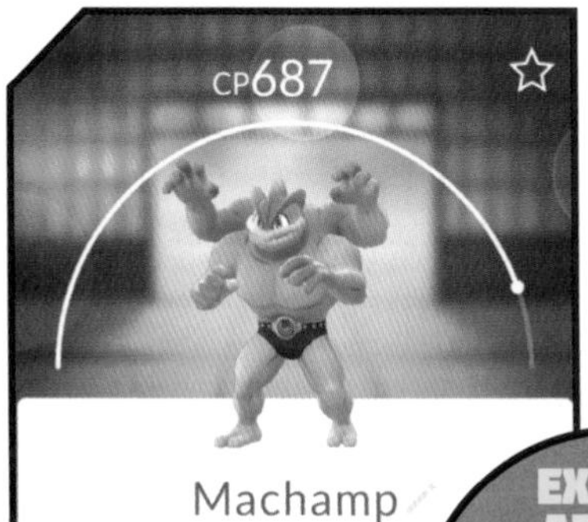

#068 MACHAMP

CLASSIFICATION Superpower pokémon
TYPE Fighting

The final evolution of the scrappy and strong Machop, Machamp has double the power of its predecessor, Machoke, thanks to four incredibly muscled arms. At the start of a battle, players can gain a fast advantage using Machamp's Bullet Punch, but they can come much closer to ensuring victory by using its special attack Stone Edge.

EXPERT ADVICE

In a gym battle, Machamp can easily overpower ice- and rock-type pokémon with similar CPs. However, as an earthly fighting pokémon, it will be weak against fairy, flying and psychic types.

#069 BELLSPROUT

CLASSIFICATION Flower pokémon
TYPE Grass/Poison

Able to replenish itself in the wild by simply rooting itself to the ground, Bellsprout can't make use of its incredible speed while rooted. Using its limbs in attacks like Vine Whip and its poison abilities by flinging an attack called Acid, Bellsprout is surprisingly effective in battle against comparable water pokémon. They can also use an attack called Wrap.

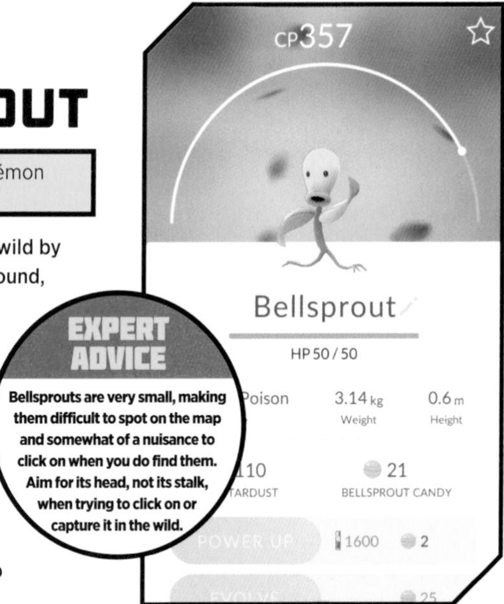

EXPERT ADVICE

Bellsprouts are very small, making them difficult to spot on the map and somewhat of a nuisance to click on when you do find them. Aim for its head, not its stalk, when trying to click on or capture it in the wild.

#070 WEEPINBELL

CLASSIFICATION Flycatcher pokémon
TYPE Grass/Poison

EXPERT ADVICE

Check the special attacks of this intermediary form between Bellsprout and Victreebell before you use it in a battle. Your best bet is to hold out for one with a strong and fast Sludge Bomb attack.

Weepinbell is the evolved version of Bellsprout, with improved poisonous capabilities as well as a larger mouth and an improved grass attack known as Power Whip that leaves water- and grass-type pokémon struggling to keep up with the life-absorbing plant. Don't try to use it against any bug types, however, or you might find your Weepinbell turning into lunch.

#071 VICTREEBEL

CLASSIFICATION Flycatcher pokémon
TYPE Grass/Poison

Victreebel's vines are definitely not just for show—wrapping its tendrils around its prey before swallowing whole is its favorite activity in the wild. After 100 Bellsprout candies, Weepinbell becomes this formidable flycatcher, whose most devastating attack is known as Solar Beam and can dry up water-type pokémon in a single blow.

EXPERT ADVICE

Despite being modeled after a venus flytrap, this grass-type pokémon is relatively ineffective against bug-type pokémon in a battle. Try using it against ground, rock and water types.

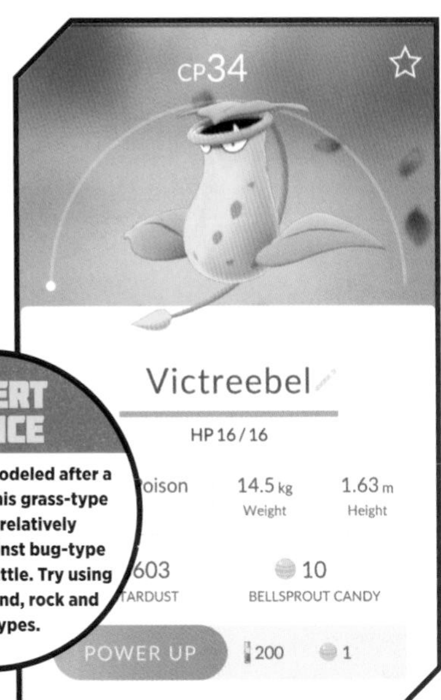

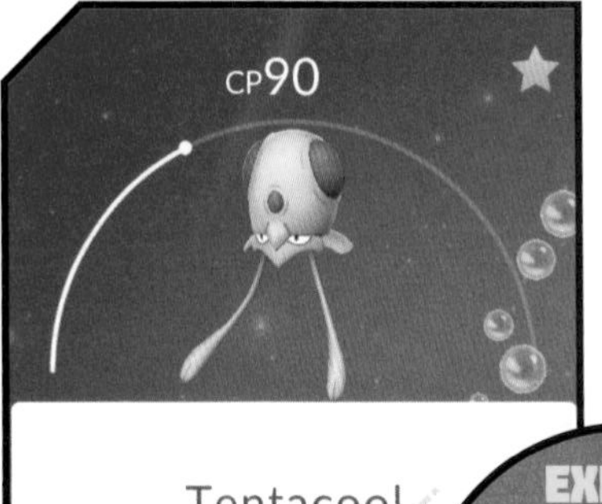

#072 TENTACOOL

CLASSIFICATION Jellyfish pokémon
TYPE Water/Poison

Like a jellyfish in real life, Tentacool is composed mostly of H_2O, but lore states it can also absorb sunlight through the two red crystals on the top of its head, powering attacks like Poison Sting, its main quick move, and special attacks like Wrap, Bubble Beam and Water Pulse. Though it becomes much more powerful after evolution, Tentacool is capable of defeating some fire types.

EXPERT ADVICE

Tentacool is pretty small, and tends to pop up disguised around water on the map. If you don't live near an ocean or pond, this pokémon can also be hatched from a 2km or a 5km egg.

#073 TENTACRUEL

CLASSIFICATION Jellyfish pokémon
TYPE Water/Poison

Tentracruel, a blue jellyfish-like pokémon with red energy-storing spheres on its head, is the final form of Tentacool. Its tentacles prove to be effective in battle, used in moves such as Acid and Poison Jab, or with attacks like Sludge Wave, which can engulf even the largest pokémon.

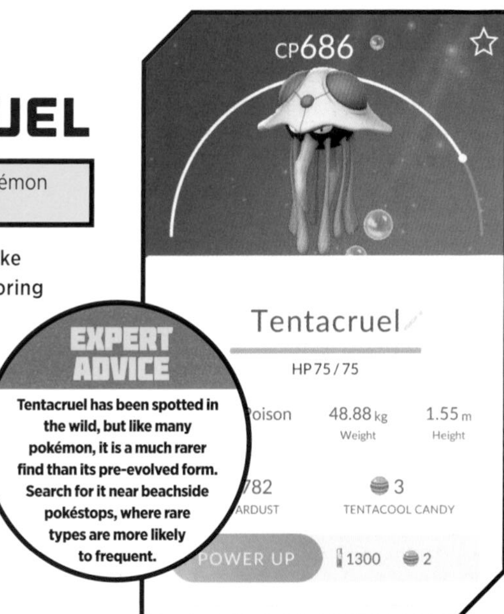

EXPERT ADVICE

Tentacruel has been spotted in the wild, but like many pokémon, it is a much rarer find than its pre-evolved form. Search for it near beachside pokéstops, where rare types are more likely to frequent.

#074 GEODUDE

CLASSIFICATION Rock pokémon
TYPE Rock/Ground

Muscular, humanoid arms ending in five-fingered hands do an incredible amount of damage despite their looks. But don't let the fists fool you—against fighting type pokémon Geodude is best left on the bench by Pokémon Go players. However, against bug, fire, flying and ice pokémon, Geodude, not all that difficult to find in the wild, could be a hidden ace in the hole.

EXPERT ADVICE

Search for Geodude in mountainous regions or near places like rock quarries, parking lots and train stations. This pokémon can also be hatched from a 2km egg.

#075 GRAVELER

CLASSIFICATION Rock pokémon
TYPE Rock/Ground

A living boulder that walks on two legs like a human, Graveler is the second evolution of Geodude, morphing after 25 Geodude candies and in turn becoming Golem after 100 Geodude candies. Pokémon Go players are wise to keep this dual-type pokémon in their roster for use against electric pokémon like Raichu. On the other hand, if you happen to be up against a steel type, leave him in the pokéball.

EXPERT ADVICE

Graveler's fast attacks can include typical rock moves like Earthquake and Tackle. Its special moves are also terrestrial, including Bulldoze, Earthquake, Rock Throw and Stone Edge.

#076 GOLEM

CLASSIFICATION Megaton pokémon
TYPE Rock/Ground

Golem can weigh in at more than 660 pounds and knows how to use every one of them in battle. Each year, Golem grows bigger after shedding its skin, becoming more and more dangerous while learning attacks like Stone Edge and Ancient Power. Just like its previous evolutions, Golem is not very effective against steel- and ground-type pokémon.

EXPERT ADVICE

Like most rock pokémon, Golem's attacks are highly effective against bug-, fire-, flying- and ice-type pokémon. It evolves from Graveler after receiving 100 Geodude candies.

#077 PONYTA

CLASSIFICATION Fire Horse pokémon
TYPE Fire

A newborn Ponyta is barely able to stand, but it learns to use the flames that lick at its entire body quickly, manipulating them into attacks like Fire Blast and Flame Charge. These can be used along with Ponyta's incredible dodging speed by Pokémon Go trainers who are looking to beef up their attacking potential against bug and grass types especially, but also ice and steel, which it can melt.

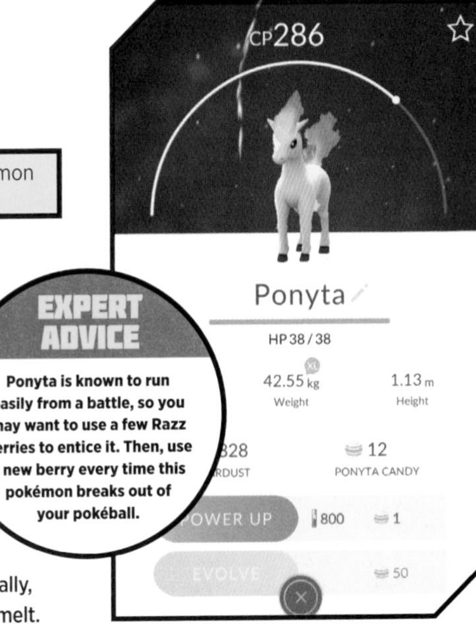

EXPERT ADVICE

Ponyta is known to run easily from a battle, so you may want to use a few Razz Berries to entice it. Then, use a new berry every time this pokémon breaks out of your pokéball.

#078 RAPIDASH

CLASSIFICATION Fire Horse pokémon
TYPE Fire

Few creatures ever win in footraces against Rapidash, who clocks in at a fleet-footed 150 mph. At full-speed, Rapidash's hooves don't even make contact with the earth as it charges toward enemies with attacks like Drill Run, Fire Blast or Heat Wave, any of which can be used to devastate grass or ice-type pokémon as well as bug types, who are especially sensitive to fire.

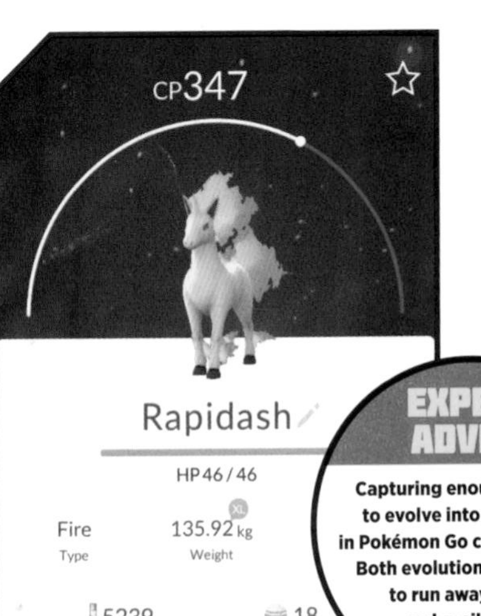

EXPERT ADVICE

Capturing enough Ponytas to evolve into a Rapidash in Pokémon Go can be difficult. Both evolutions are known to run away quickly and easily from a capture.

#079 SLOWPOKE

CLASSIFICATION Dopey pokémon
TYPE Water/Psychic

Slowpoke uses its long tail as a lure, which eventually becomes the host for a Shellder after 50 candies when Slowpoke evolves into Slowbro. Its most effective move is Water Pulse, an upgraded version of its basic ability Water Gun, which can be effective against certain fire and ground pokémon, despite the Slowpoke's reputation as a relatively lazy pokémon.

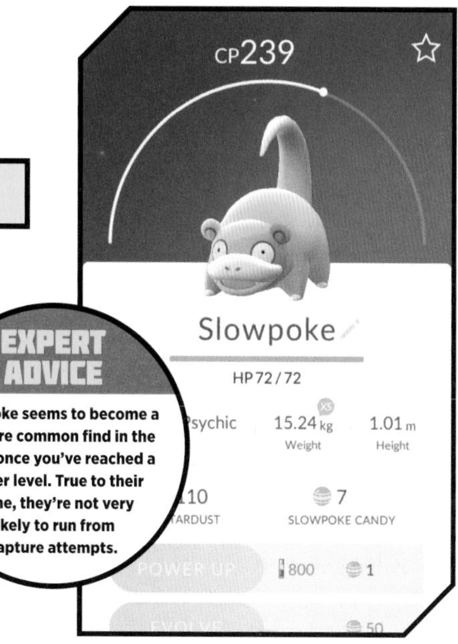

EXPERT ADVICE

Slowpoke seems to become a far more common find in the game once you've reached a higher level. True to their name, they're not very likely to run from capture attempts.

#080 SLOWBRO

CLASSIFICATION Hermit Crab pokémon
TYPE Water/Psychic

The Shellder attached to a Slowbro's tail is the catalyst for a symbiotic relationship that turns the lazy pokémon into a true fighter. Adding psychic abilities to the water attacks preferred by Slowpoke, Slowbro can be used by Pokémon Go trainers against fighting and poison pokémon, who may be surprised at being beaten by Slowbro.

EXPERT ADVICE

Slowbro packs a combination of water-, psychic- and ice-type attacks. It's commonly found hanging out near canals, docks, harbors and ship ports.

#081 MAGNEMITE

CLASSIFICATION Magnet pokémon
TYPE Electric/Steel

With the help of its magnets, Magnemite is able to defy gravity, which is useful in battle for obvious reasons. Its electric currents can destroy even the most imposing water pokémon under the right circumstances, so Magnemite is a useful find if you're planning on attacking any gyms with high-CP water monsters guarding it.

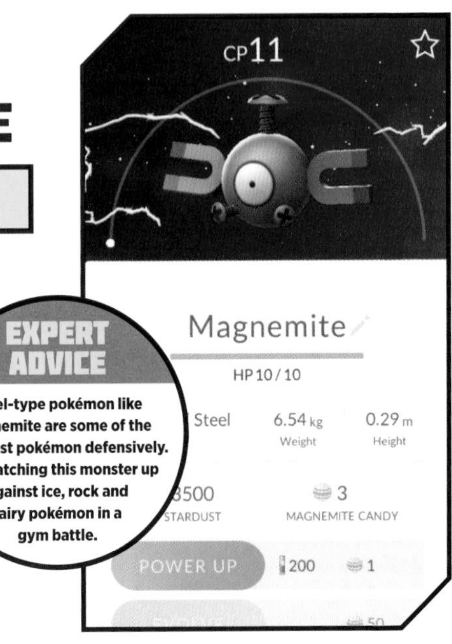

EXPERT ADVICE

Steel-type pokémon like Magnemite are some of the strongest pokémon defensively. Try matching this monster up against ice, rock and fairy pokémon in a gym battle.

#082 MAGNETON

CLASSIFICATION Magnet pokémon
TYPE Electric/Steel

After 50 Magnemite candies, the magnetic oddball triples itself into Magneton, which can turn electric energy into tangible barriers with attacks like Thunder Shock. Just like its previous evolution, Magneton is wonderful against water types, but beware of grass and ground pokémon that are resistant to its electric energy. These will steamroll over your Magneton.

EXPERT ADVICE

Magneton (and other steel-type pokémon) are not very effective against fire or electric types in a battle, so be sure not to line them up with any Pikachus or Charizards at the gym.

#083 FARFETCH'D

CLASSIFICATION Wild Duck pokémon
TYPE Normal/Flying

Always carrying an onion stalk that it will protect with its life, Farfetch'd uses it for everything from food to self defense. The moves Aerial Ace, Air Cutter and Leaf Blade make up the arsenal at Farfetch'd's disposal, but beware: As a normal type pokémon, it isn't effective against any one type more than another, and it is particularly weak against fighting types.

EXPERT ADVICE

So far, spotting a Farfetch'd in the wild has been very rare, except in Asia. When people do find this "regional rare" on their maps, this pokémon is known to run away, so act fast if you see one!

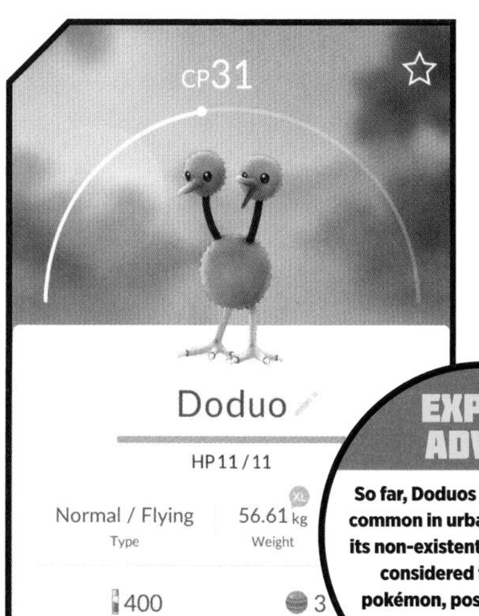

#084 DODUO

CLASSIFICATION Twin Bird pokémon
TYPE Normal/Flying

Doduo can be useful in battle with its twin beaks, both razor sharp, and its legs which can carry it up to 60 mph. Using a special move known as Drill Peck, the two-headed bird makes an interesting opponent in Pokémon Go. Pitting a relatively high CP Doduo against a bug-type pokémon, even one as intimidating as Pinsir, could yield results for the bold pokémon master.

EXPERT ADVICE

So far, Doduos seem to be very common in urban areas. Despite its non-existent wings, Doduo is considered to be a flying pokémon, possibly hinting at hidden attributes under its plumage.

#085 DODRIO

CLASSIFICATION Triple Bird pokémon
TYPE Normal/Flying

After 50 Doduo candies, Doduo evolves into this three-headed avian, which pokémon lore says has three different personalities to go along with each individual cranium. The three heads give Dodrio an incredible Feint attack, which Pokémon Go trainers can use to gain the upper hand early in battles. Afterwards, Drill Peck or Air Cutter can demolish enemies with ease.

EXPERT ADVICE

Flying-type pokémon like Dodrio are super effective against bug, fighting and grass pokémon. But watch out: An electric pokémon can knock them out of the arena and defeat them quickly.

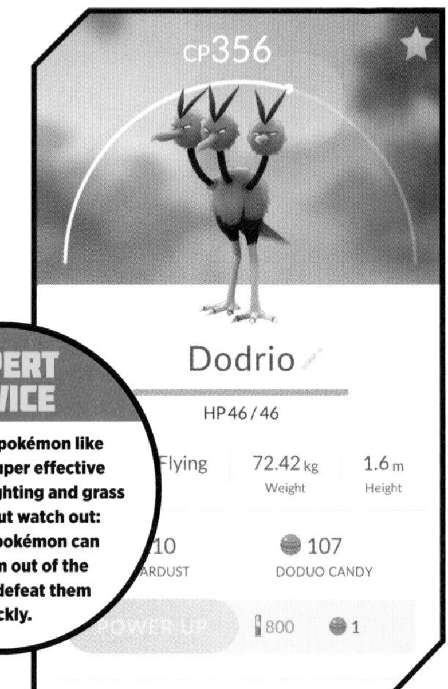

#086 SEEL

CLASSIFICATION Sea Lion pokémon
TYPE Water

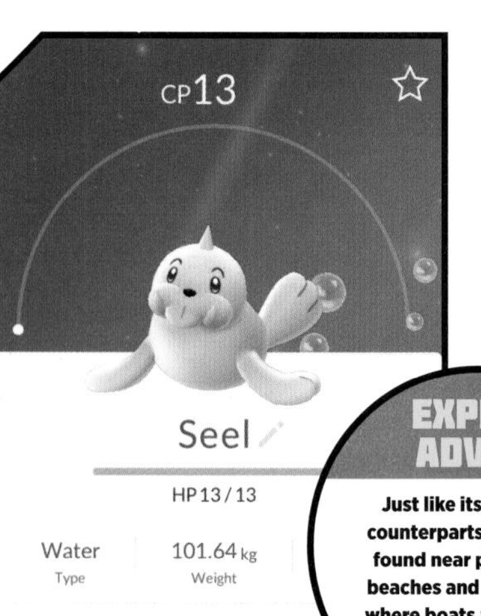

Seel uses the horn on its forehead in battle along with strong tusks that it can also use to break through ice. Most effective against fire, ground and rock types, Seel's Icy Wind attack leaves enemies with a distinctly less cuddly impression than its appearance. Its quick attacks are Ice Shard and Water Gun, either of which are enough to extinguish a Charmander's flame.

EXPERT ADVICE

Just like its real-world counterparts, Seel can be found near piers, docks, beaches and other places where boats are common. They seem to be relatively rare out in the wild.

#087 DEWGONG

CLASSIFICATION Sea Lion pokémon
TYPE Water/Ice

Able to keep a precise body heat even in the most unbearably cold temperatures, Dewgongs actually regain power during terrible weather like hailstorms according to Pokémon lore. After evolving from Seel, Dewgong gains the possible special move Blizzard, which expands on the Icy Wind theme and can be used in battle to snuff out fire and ground types.

EXPERT ADVICE

Dewgong evolves from Seel after collecting 50 Seel candies. Like other ice-type pokémon, its attacks are also super effective against dragon, flying and grass types in a gym battle.

#088 GRIMER

CLASSIFICATION Sludge pokémon
TYPE Poison

EXPERT ADVICE

Try searching for Grimer and other poison types in damp, sticky places like moors or bogs. This pokémon's relatively large size also makes it easy to catch with a pokéball out in the wild.

Able to squeeze through any hole or crevice due to their complete lack of a formal shape or bone structure, Grimer is also highly toxic, using a simple Mud Slap to spread its poison to enemies in gym battles. If a charge attack is required, Grimer can demolish fairy and grass types with Sludge Bomb, Sludge or Mud Bomb depending on your level and your Grimer's CP.

#089 MUK

CLASSIFICATION Sludge pokémon
TYPE Poison

After 50 Grimer candies, the amorphous blob of sludge becomes Muk, which immediately kills anything in its path with deadly poison delivered by the quick attacks Acid and Poison Jab, both of which prove to fairy- and grass-type pokémon that Muk is a great deal more malevolent than Grimer. That doesn't mean it can't be beaten however. Try a psychic-type pokémon.

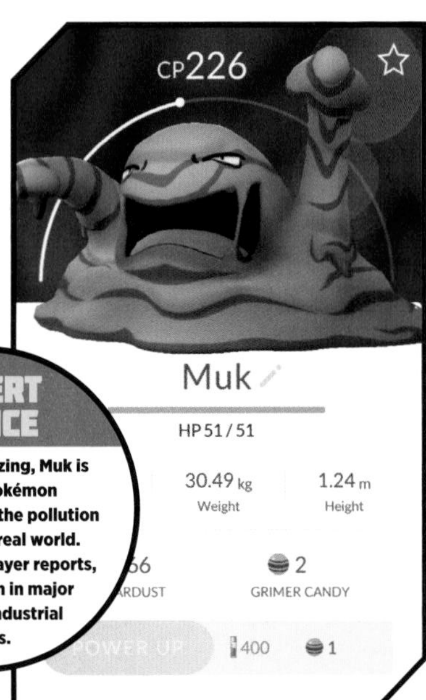

EXPERT ADVICE

Similar to Weezing, Muk is a virtual pokémon embodiment of the pollution affecting the real world. According to player reports, he is common in major cities and industrial areas.

#090 SHELLDER

CLASSIFICATION Bivalve pokémon
TYPE Water/Psychic

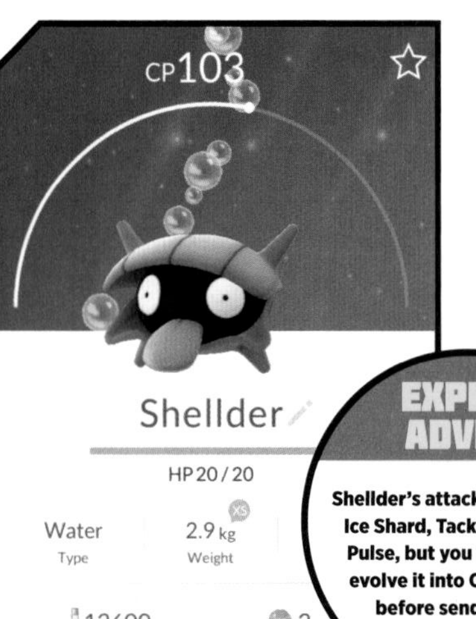

Shellder is most useful as a collection piece until you can evolve it at the right time into a Cloyster, but if you find yourself in battle against one of these tricky little shells, it's useful to know that any of your dragon- or grass-type pokémon will have an easy time defending attacks like Bubble Beam and will even be able to withstand Icy Wind most of the time.

EXPERT ADVICE

Shellder's attacks also include Ice Shard, Tackle and Water Pulse, but you may want to evolve it into Cloyster first before sending it off to battle.

#091 CLOYSTER

CLASSIFICATION Bivalve pokémon
TYPE Water/Ice

Cloyster is capable of attacking any enemy without ever opening its shell and exposing itself to easy hits from its opponent. It first likes to debilitate enemies with the quick attack Frost Breath before finishing them off with either Blizzard, Icy Wind or Hydro Pump. If you have a high CP electric type in your roster, Cloyster is a good opponent to test them out against.

EXPERT ADVICE

Like other water pokémon, Cloyster's attacks are super effective against fire, ground and rock pokémon. However, it is weak against dragon, grass and other water types in battle.

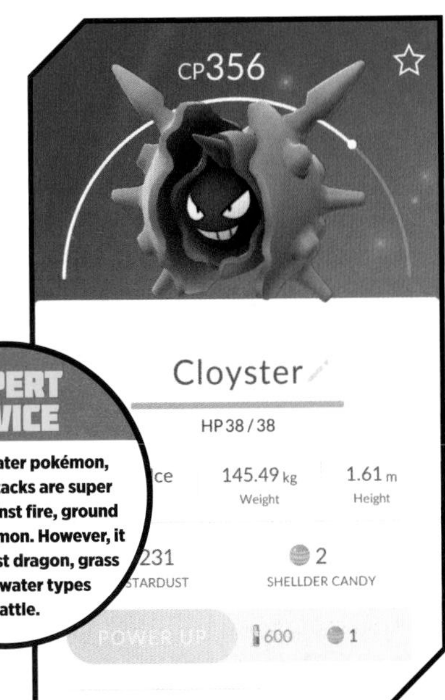

#092 GASTLY

CLASSIFICATION Gas pokémon
TYPE Ghost/Poison

A frightening pokémon to spot, especially in battle, Gastly is a welcome addition to any trainer's pokédex. Gastly loves to use its tongue for a quick attack, but is weak against fairy and fighting pokémon. Ideally, you want to get a Gastly capable of performing the Sludge Bomb special move, a poison-type attack that puts the hurt on fairy- and grass-type pokémon.

EXPERT ADVICE

Look for Gastly, the classic ghost pokémon, at night. Contrary to popular myths, Gastly and other spooks are not more likely to appear in cemeteries, so show some respect.

#093 HAUNTER

CLASSIFICATION Gas pokémon
TYPE Ghost/Poison

After 25 Gastly candies, it becomes Haunter, a terrifying creature that according to Pokémon lore is more evil than the mischief-loving Gastly. Using Shadow Ball, Sludge Bomb or Dark Pulse, Haunter takes pleasure in demolishing other ghost pokémon, as well as any creature who tries to lure it with psychic tricks. It's difficult to match up, but a high CP ground type is a good bet.

EXPERT ADVICE

Due to its unique type combination, Haunter and its other evolved forms are the only ghost-type pokémon in the game that are weak against psychic-type moves in a battle.

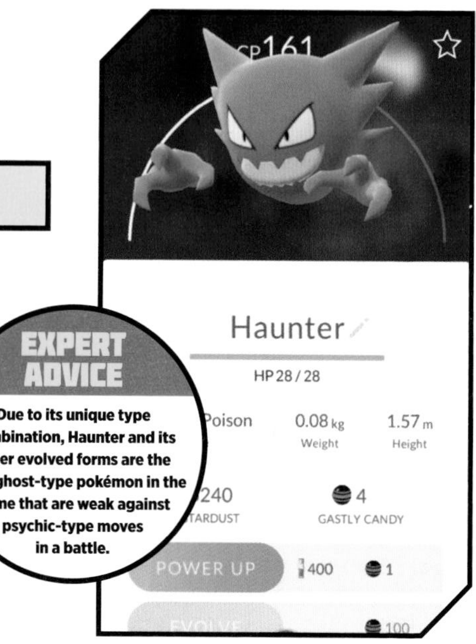

#094 GENGAR

CLASSIFICATION Shadow pokémon
TYPE Ghost/Poison

Evolving from Haunter after 100 Gastly candies, Gengar can change shape, adding another dimension of danger to the attacks Sludge Wave and Shadow Ball, which it adds to Haunter's repertoire after evolution. Whatever you do, don't try to go into battle against Gengar with another ghost type unless you're wildly undermatched in CP.

EXPERT ADVICE

Gengars often appear in the wild at night in cities. Like other ghost pokémon, its attacks are super effective against other ghost types in battle, but may not be a good match against normal types.

#095 ONIX

CLASSIFICATION Rock Snake pokémon
TYPE Rock/Ground

Able to tunnel and bore at a speed of more than 50 miles an hour, Onix is extremely aggressive and uses every bit of its momentum in its attacks. These are Tackle, which sounds more innocent than the freight-train it is, Rock Throw, Iron Head, Rock Slide and Stone Edge. Unsurprisingly, Onix has the best time squashing high-level bug pokémon into oblivion.

EXPERT ADVICE

Onix can be a little bit tricky to catch in the wild because it essentially fills up the entire phone screen with its massive rock body. Aim for the colored circle and don't get distracted!

#096 DROWZEE

CLASSIFICATION Hypnosis pokémon
TYPE Psychic

According to Pokémon lore, Drowzee's ability to hypnotize people into a deep sleep and then sense their dreams is its greatest strength. The psychic quick attack that achieves this is called Confusion, which can be used instead of Pound, its normal ability. Though its charge attacks Psychic, Psybeam and Psyshock can inflict heavy damage, collecting candies and evolving your Drowzee into a Hypno will yield the best results.

EXPERT ADVICE

Drowzees are common in urban areas. Like most psychic pokémon, its strong mind is very effective against fighting and poison pokémon. Ghost pokémon are its main weakness.

#097 HYPNO

CLASSIFICATION Hypnosis pokémon
TYPE Psychic

After 50 Drowzee candies, the elephant-faced Dream Eater evolves into Hypno, a much more powerful pokémon with attacks such as Zen Headbutt, Shadow Ball, Psyshock and Confusion. This psychic-type pokémon is a great gym defender, turning even the most powerful monsters into putty using nothing but its mind.

EXPERT ADVICE

Psychic-type pokemon like Hypno are especially weak against Ghost types in a gym battle. You'll want to search for both of these types together at night, when they are more likely to spawn.

#098 KRABBY

CLASSIFICATION River Crab pokémon
TYPE Water

Krabby burrows in the sand both to make its nest and to stalk prey, and it has the ability to regenerate damaged or lost claws, which comes in handy after its attacks, Mudshot and Vice Grip go horribly awry. Smaller fire pokémon are very sensitive to Krabby's water-based attacks, but its main purpose is evolving into Kingler with enough candies. Just look at that claw, after all.

EXPERT ADVICE

This pokémon is exceedingly common in locations where there is water nearby. After collecting 50 Krabby candies, you can cash in and evolve it to Kingler, a much more powerful crab.

#099 KINGLER

CLASSIFICATION Pincer pokémon
TYPE Water

When Krabby collects 50 candies, it gets massive claws that extend from the hips of its new form, Kingler, with the left one weighing in at double the size of the right. With a quick attack called Metal Claw, Kingler can slowly wear away at the defenses of even the most massive fire pokémon and follow up with the charge attacks X-Scissor, Vice Grip and Water Pulse.

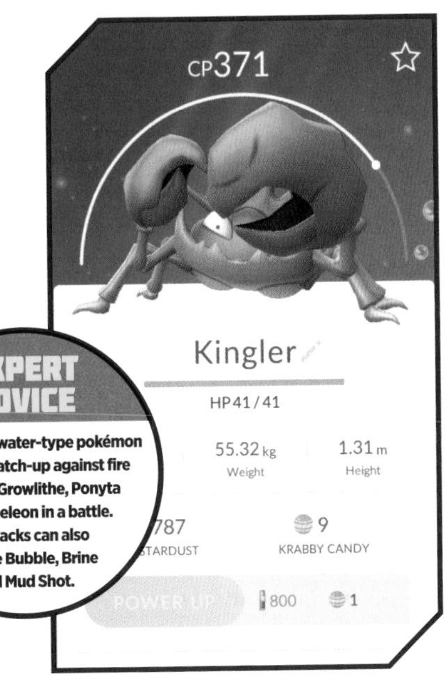

EXPERT ADVICE

This massive water-type pokémon is a great match-up against fire types like Growlithe, Ponyta or Charmeleon in a battle. Its attacks can also include Bubble, Brine and Mud Shot.

#100 VOLTORB

CLASSIFICATION Ball pokémon
TYPE Electric

Voltorb was originally discovered in a pokéball factory, so take this mechanical theme to its logical conclusion with the devastating electric attacks Spark and Tackle, which pound enemies into oblivion as charge attacks Thunderbolt, Signal Beam and Discharge warm up. Just don't send one into battle against rock or ground pokémon.

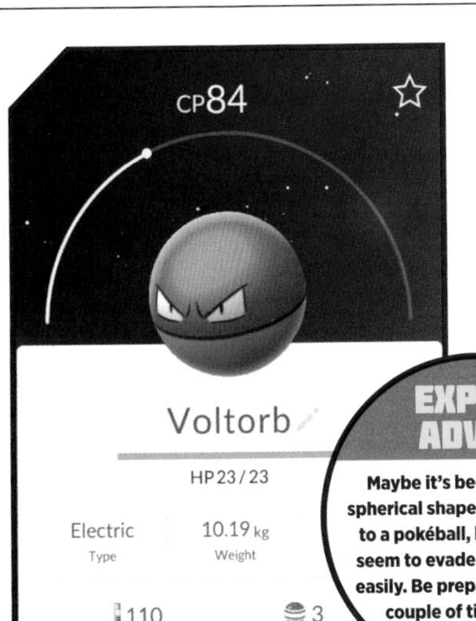

EXPERT ADVICE

Maybe it's because of their spherical shape and similar size to a pokéball, but these guys seem to evade capture pretty easily. Be prepared to throw a couple of times before you catch it.

#101 ELECTRODE

CLASSIFICATION Ball pokémon
TYPE Electric

Adding the charge attack Hyper Beam to Voltorb's formidable arsenal of electric attacks, Electrode is super effective against flying and water-type pokémon, who are respectively plucked from the sky and sizzled by the pokéball-resembling menace. If you're unlucky enough to battle one, make sure you have a ground-type pokémon like Marowak in your roster to neutralize the electricity.

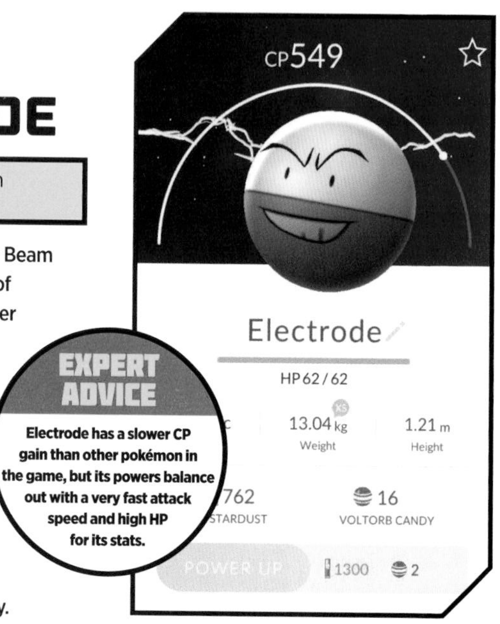

EXPERT ADVICE

Electrode has a slower CP gain than other pokémon in the game, but its powers balance out with a very fast attack speed and high HP for its stats.

CP373
Exeggcute
HP 58 / 58
Grass / Psychic
Type
2.46 kg
Weight
110
STARDUST
19
EXEGGCUTE CANDY
POWER UP
1600
2
EVOLVE
50

#102 EXEGGCUTE

CLASSIFICATION Egg pokémon
TYPE Grass/Psychic

Despite its chicken-egg appearance, Exeggcute is more closely related to plant seeds, with each group consisting of six parts (five whole parts around an exposed "yolk" in the center). Exeggcute's main battle strategy is to confound its enemies, biding time and escaping until it can evolve into its much stronger final form, the palm tree-like Exeggutor.

EXPERT ADVICE

Ironically, Exeggcute can be hatched from an egg if you're willing to walk a few kilometers. In the wild, it can also be found most commonly in suburban and urban areas where grass is plentiful.

#103 EXEGGUTOR

CLASSIFICATION Coconut pokémon
TYPE Grass/Psychic

After collecting 50 Exeggcute candies, the strange egg-like pokémon becomes the much more unified and formidable Exeggutor, capable of devastating grass attacks as well as psychic standby attacks like Zen Headbutt. Useful in battles thanks to its size and its variety of moves, Exeggutor is worth the amount of time it will take collecting the decidedly unglamorous Exeggcute.

EXPERT ADVICE

Exeggutor is one of the highest ranked plant-type pokemon in the game, especially when considering its hidden IV stats. Specifically, its psychic attacks are some of the strongest of its kind.

#104 CUBONE

CLASSIFICATION Lonely pokémon
TYPE Ground

Cubone is one of the smartest pokémon in your roster and survives thanks to the use of a bone club it carries, attacking with Bone Club and Bonemerang, which deploy the club to deadly use. Capable of both ground and fighting attacks, Cubone is extremely useful against fire and poison types, despite its relatively meager HP and CP indexes.

EXPERT ADVICE

Cubones will appear to lower-level trainers and are relatively easy to catch once engaged. They also almost never run from a capturing attempt, so rest easy if you end up finding one.

#105 MAROWAK

CLASSIFICATION Bone Keeper pokémon
TYPE Ground

Feeding Cubone 50 candies evolves the pokémon into Marowak, an even more capable fighter using even more fearsome skill with its beloved bone staff. Almost all of Marowak's possible moves will be ground type, so don't expect a lot of variety in the type of attacks it can launch on opponents.

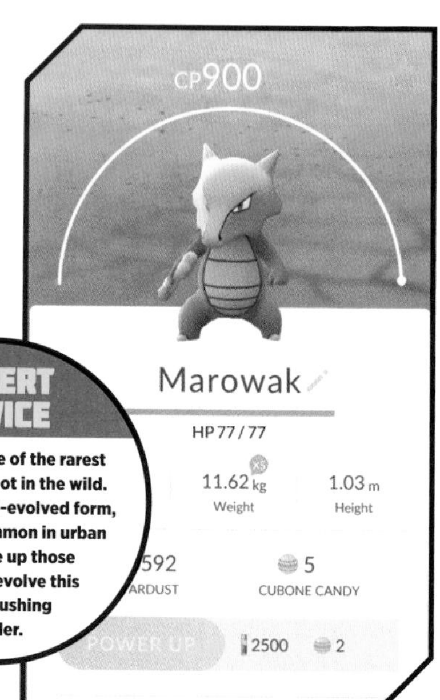

EXPERT ADVICE

Marowak is one of the rarest pokémon to spot in the wild. However, its pre-evolved form, Cubone, is common in urban areas. Save up those candies to evolve this bone-crushing battler.

#106 HITMONLEE

CLASSIFICATION Kicking pokémon
TYPE Fighting

What's more terrifying than a torso with eyes? A torso with eyes and a killer kick. Hitmonlee's name references the great martial artist Bruce Lee, who also performed amazing feats with his feet. But it is not the pedigree of the pokémon's name that makes it a favorite with players—it's how effective the pokémon is in battle.

EXPERT ADVICE

Hitmonlee has been spotted in a variety of cities, but be prepared for a difficult fight should you find it. Its possible attacks for gym battles include Rock Smash, Stone Edge and Stomp.

#107 HITMONCHAN

CLASSIFICATION Punching pokémon
TYPE Fighting

In the Pokémon universe, Hitmonchan is a species related to Hitmonlee that specializes in punching and has the style to match, appearing to always wear a purple athletic tunic and red boxing gloves. This pugilist pokémon will end up having one of three special moves—Fire Punch, Ice Punch or Thunder Punch.

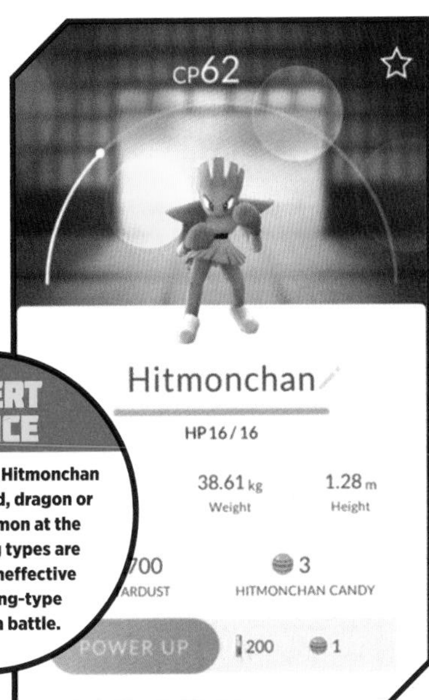

EXPERT ADVICE

Be careful using Hitmonchan against any bird, dragon or bat-like pokémon at the gym. Fighting types are notoriously ineffective against flying-type pokémon in battle.

#108 LICKITUNG

CLASSIFICATION Licking pokémon
TYPE Normal

This pokémon may look more suited to taking out a gallon of ice cream than rival fighters, but don't judge a book by its cover. According to Pokémon lore, Lickitung's tongue measures at more than six feet long, and trainers in Pokémon Go have discovered it is a potent weapon. If you face one in battle, don't make the mistake of underestimating its power!

EXPERT ADVICE

Lickitung's signature special attack, Lick, takes a very long time to charge up in battle. However, if you can afford to wait, it's a powerful move that can wipe out a pokémon in one wet swipe.

#109 KOFFING

CLASSIFICATION Poison Gas pokémon
TYPE Poison

A spherical pokémon that, according to Pokémon lore, is made from toxic gas, Koffing is a disgusting yet effective pokémon. Fans of the Pokémon anime may have a soft spot in their heart for Koffing (and its evolved form, Weezing), as it was a favorite of Team Rocket member James. One way to add it to your team is to get lucky and hatch it from a 5km egg.

EXPERT ADVICE

Koffings are a relatively rare find in many regions, but they have been spotted in the suburbs, often at polluted places like parking lots, industrial zones or dumping sites.

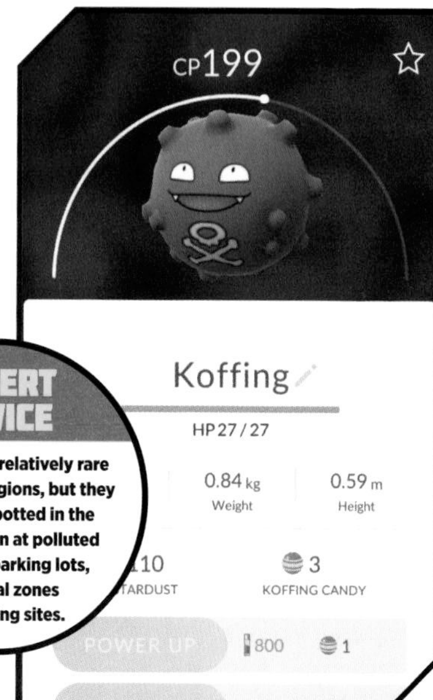

#110 WEEZING

CLASSIFICATION Poison Gas pokémon
TYPE Poison

EXPERT ADVICE

Weezing is an incredible counter against fighting-type pokémon like Hitmonlee and Hitmonchan in a gym battle. Its special charge attacks can include Sludge Bomb, Sludge, Smog and Tackle.

Weezing, the evolved form of Koffing, is a purple pokémon with two heads for twice the trouble. This poison-type pokémon may tear apart grass and fairy-type pokémon with relative ease, but it runs into trouble when confronted by ground or psychic pokémon. In pokémon lore, it goes through household trash at night, but Pokémon Go doesn't force you to dumpster dive for this pokémon.

#111 RHYHORN

CLASSIFICATION Spikes pokémon
TYPE Ground/rock

This large, rock-like pokémon is a great pokémon to have in your pokédex. Rhyhorn is a fearless fighter and its nature shows in special moves such as Bulldoze and Horn Attack. Even better for trainers, Rhyhorn will evolve into an even more fearsome form after you feed it 50 candies.

EXPERT ADVICE

If Rhyhorn is uncommon in your area, know you can also evolve it from a 5km egg. Its attacks in Pokémon Go can also include Earthquake, Drill Run and Take Down.

#112 RHYDON

CLASSIFICATION Spikes pokémon
TYPE Ground

EXPERT ADVICE

Search for Rhydon and other rock-type pokémon in places where "stone" is a regular feature, such as parking lots, quarries, train stations or large buildings such as shopping malls.

Sporting spikes, a horn, a tail and tough armor, Rhydon is a formidable opponent in the gym. Trainers should be mindful, however, that the ground-type Rhydon is vulnerable to water-type attacks, commonly used among the water-type pokémon that tend to dominate gyms in many coastal areas.

#113 CHANSEY

CLASSIFICATION Egg pokémon
TYPE Normal

In Pokémon lore, there are not male Chansey pokémon. Instead, every member of the species is born a female with a dark pink egg pouch and lays several eggs a day. In Pokémon Go, Chansey follows the lore by being a rare find for trainers, but it is definitely worth the trouble. Chansey has one of the best HP scores in the game, even if it has a low CP overall.

EXPERT ADVICE

Chansey is a great defender but also a rare find. Only more experienced trainers (Level 7 and higher) will encounter it in the wild. You can also hatch Chansey from a 10km egg.

#114 TANGELA

CLASSIFICATION Vine pokémon
TYPE Grass

Covered with soft blue vines, only Tangela's feet and eyes are visible. While most of its moves are grass type (as you would expect), it's possible for this tangled pokémon to learn Sludge Bomb as a special move, which is a poison-type attack effective against fairy and grass pokémon alike.

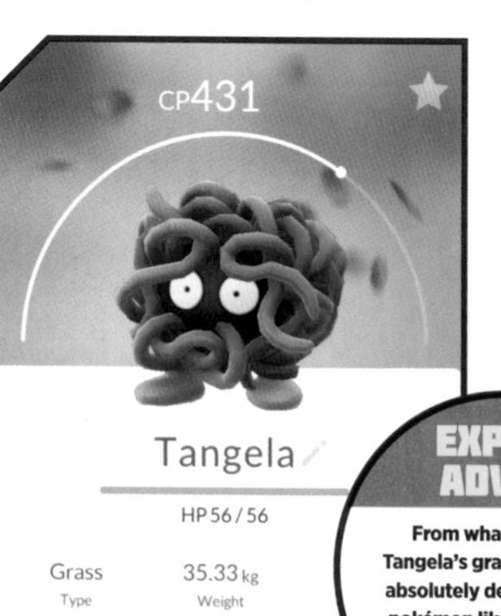

EXPERT ADVICE

From what I've seen, Tangela's grass attacks can absolutely destroy a water pokémon like Starmie in a rival gym battle, even if it has half the CP.

#115 KANGASKHAN

CLASSIFICATION Parent pokémon
TYPE Normal

A massive biped with a heavy, blunt tail that can be used as a weapon if necessary, Kangaskhan is a heavy hitter that any Pokémon Go player would be thrilled to have in the pokédex. While it is a normal-type pokémon, Kangaskhan also can possibly possess fighting and ground-type attacks as well.

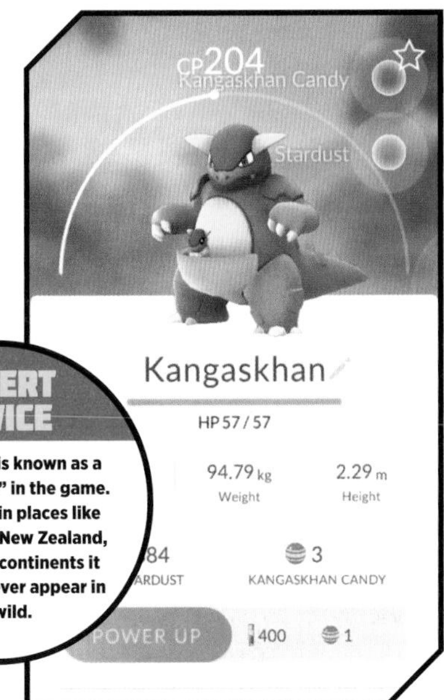

EXPERT ADVICE

Kangaskhan is known as a "regional rare" in the game. It's common in places like Australia and New Zealand, but on other continents it will almost never appear in the wild.

#116 HORSEA

CLASSIFICATION Dragon pokémon
TYPE Water

EXPERT ADVICE

Horsea can be found near lakes, rivers and streams. For such a small pokémon, it can have some big special attacks, including Dragon Breath, Dragon Pulse and Hydro Pump.

One of the most able swimmers in the pokémon world, Horsea can use its dorsal fin to propel it in any direction while facing forward. Its tail can be used to anchor it to a convenient post or to balance in choppy water. Among this little guy's possible special moves is Flash Cannon, which is a steel-type attack despite Horsea being a water type.

#117 SEADRA

CLASSIFICATION Dragon pokémon
TYPE Water

Seadras are the evolved form of Horsea pokémon. They look very much like seahorses, with lower pectoral fins that have sharp points and exude venom in Pokémon lore (though Pokémon Go players will notice Seadra can't perform any poison-type attacks). Seadras don't evolve into a higher form, but still manage to pack quite a punch in battle.

EXPERT ADVICE

Seadras will be common wherever you find their pre-evolved form Horsea but like many final evolutions, they are likely to appear more commonly among higher-level trainers.

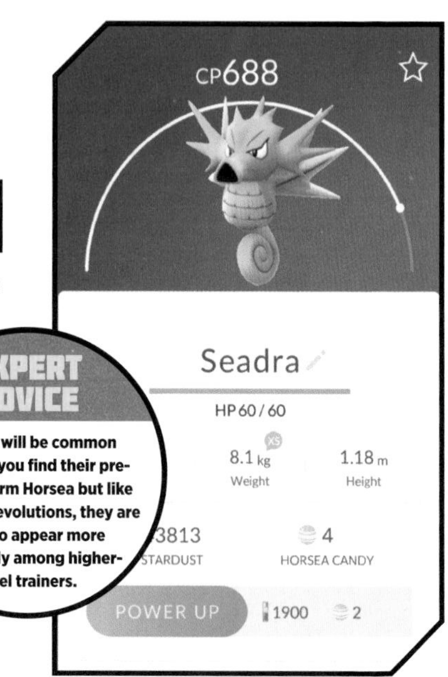

#118 GOLDEEN

CLASSIFICATION Goldfish pokémon
TYPE Water

What looks to be a cross between a goldfish and a unicorn, Goldeen is a common water-type pokémon found by players of Pokémon Go who spend time around bodies of water. Although its home is in the water, Goldeen is also able to perform Peck, a flying-type attack. It also puts its horn to use with the normal-type move Horn Attack.

EXPERT ADVICE

Goldeens are relatively easy to catch in the game compared to other pokémon. While this fish isn't necessarily powerful in a gym battle, its evolved form, Seaking, is a coveted prize among trainers.

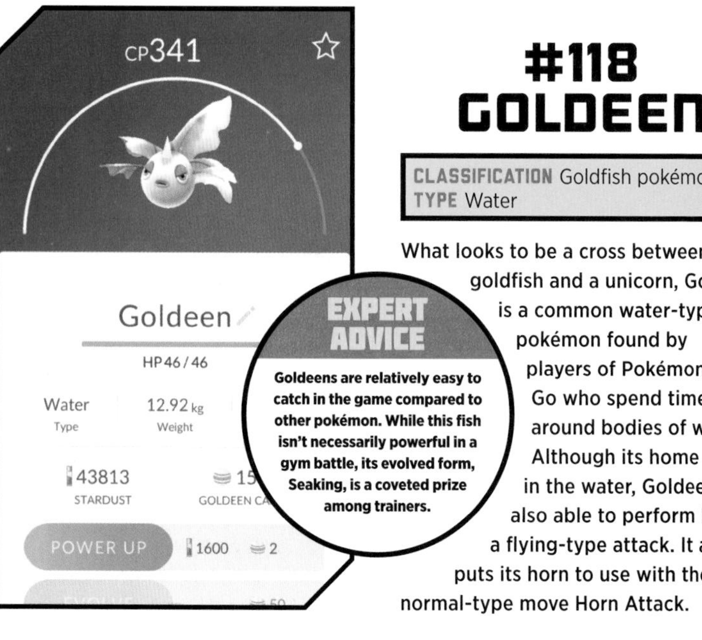

#119 SEAKING

CLASSIFICATION Goldfish pokémon
TYPE Water

Prized among Pokémon Go players, this black, white and orange speckled fish pokémon with a horn and two prominent teeth can perform attacks of many different types depending on what moves it ends up with. Drill Run, Icy Wind and Megahorn are all possible special moves, and are ground, ice and bug type, respectively.

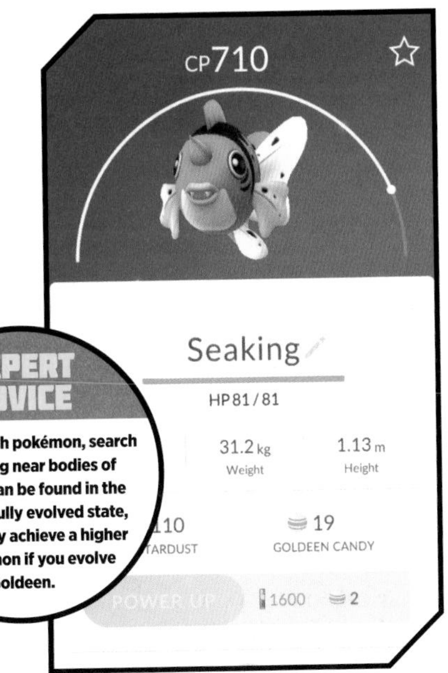

EXPERT ADVICE

As with all fish pokémon, search for Seaking near bodies of water. He can be found in the wild in his fully evolved state, but you may achieve a higher CP pokémon if you evolve Goldeen.

#120 STARYU

CLASSIFICATION Star Shape pokémon
TYPE Water

This otherwise unremarkable pokémon is capable of evolving into the formidable Starmie provided you feed it 50 candies. As you might expect of a pokémon resembling a starfish, Staryu is capable of performing both water-type and rock-type attacks, such as Bubble Beam and Power Gem, respectively.

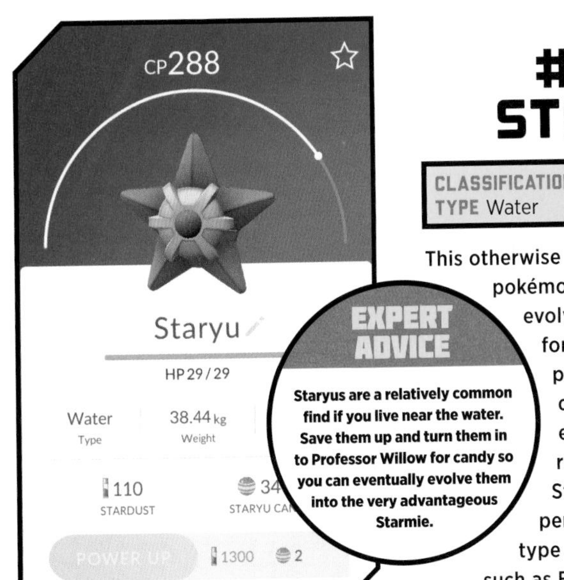

EXPERT ADVICE

Staryus are a relatively common find if you live near the water. Save them up and turn them in to Professor Willow for candy so you can eventually evolve them into the very advantageous Starmie.

#121 STARMIE

CLASSIFICATION Mysterious pokémon
TYPE Water

Nicknamed "the gem of the sea," in Pokémon lore, Starmie has seven purple limbs and a gemstone in its center. Because of its species stats and possible attacks, Starmie is a popular pokémon for trainers wanting to dominate Pokémon Go's gym battle scene. That's a pokémon worth catching.

EXPERT ADVICE

In a battle, Starmie's dodge feels very snappy, so make sure to try it out in a battle. If you're lucky to find one with a Water Gun attack, even better. The fast attack is great to use while its special charges up.

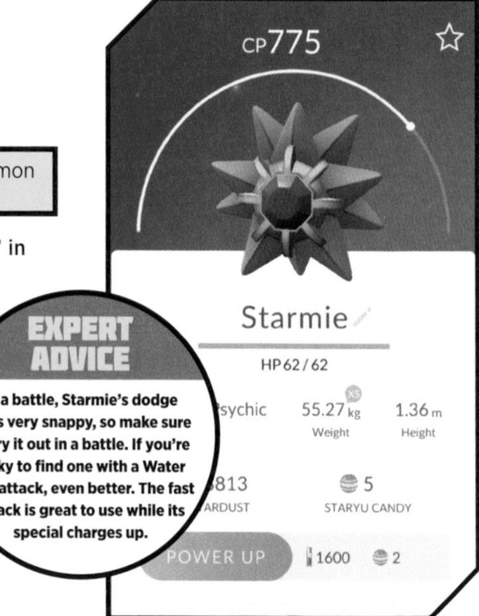

#122 MR. MIME

CLASSIFICATION Barrier pokémon
TYPE Psychic

In the Pokémon universe, this rare pokémon sometimes shows up in suburban areas performing its odd routine, punishing those who interrupt its performance with a powerful slap (a violent mime? Terrifying.) Mr. Mime happens to be one of 14 pokémon in the game capable of performing ghost-type moves, making it a monster capable of rare feats for its trainer in battle.

EXPERT ADVICE

Mr. Mime is another "regional rare" in the Pokémon Go universe. It is common in places like France and other countries in western Europe, but tough to find in other locations.

#123 SCYTHER

CLASSIFICATION Mantis pokémon
TYPE Bug/Flying

A bipedal, green insect-like pokémon, Scyther predictably attacks opponents with a variety of bug-type moves, which can include Fury Cutter, Bug Buzz and X-Scissor. Because Scyther doesn't have a more powerful form to evolve into, trainers can power it up without feeling guilty.

EXPERT ADVICE

He may look really cool, but as a combined grass/bug-type pokémon, Scyther has a lot of weaknesses in battle. Try not to use it against fire, flying, rock, ghost, steel, poison or fairy pokémon.

#124 JYNX

CLASSIFICATION Human Shape pokémon
TYPE Ice/Psychic

Never seen without the red gown that covers both its legs and feet, Jynx is an almost human-looking pokémon possessing psychic abilities and a talent for dance. Jynx is also one of the few ice-type pokémon in Pokémon Go that trainers have spotted so far, and its possible attacks include a variety of types—ice, fairy, psychic and normal.

EXPERT ADVICE

As a psychic type, Jynx is apparently a very tricky pokémon to catch out in the wild, but has been spotted in a variety of locales. This pokémon can also be hatched from a 10km egg.

#125 ELECTABUZZ

CLASSIFICATION Electric pokémon
TYPE Electric

The lightning-bolt stripe across its chest makes it clear to any observors Electabuzz is a pokémon that relies on electrical powers to prevail in battle and to protect itself from aggressors. As a result, almost all of this pokémon's attacks are electric type, with the exception of Low Kick, which is a fast, fighting-type attack.

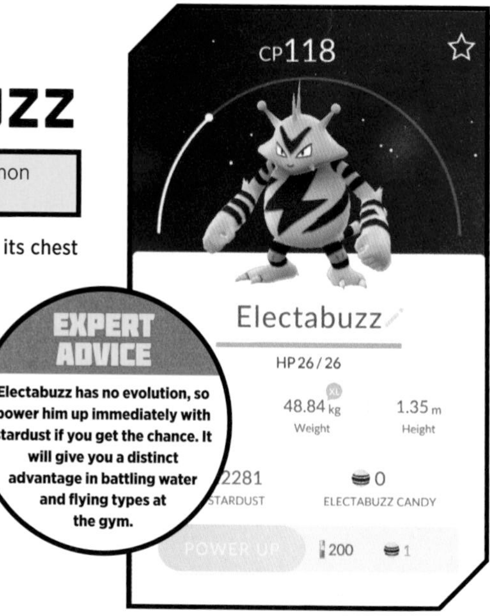

EXPERT ADVICE

Electabuzz has no evolution, so power him up immediately with stardust if you get the chance. It will give you a distinct advantage in battling water and flying types at the gym.

#126 MAGMAR

CLASSIFICATION Spitfire pokémon
TYPE Fire

Its puckered yellowed beak might make Magmar look like a duck, but this bold-looking pokémon is a handy monster to use in certain gym battles. Its Fire Blast and Fire Punch attacks can make quick work of any grass-type pokémon, making it a valuable part of the team when assaulting a gym defended by a Venusaur.

EXPERT ADVICE

Magmar can be hatched via a 10km egg or found near dry, hot places, such as deserts, rocky mountains and beaches. Like other fire types, it is also a great battle counter to steel types.

#127 PINSIR

CLASSIFICATION Stagbeetle pokémon
TYPE Bug

Pinsir's massive pincers are deployed to mangle opponents in a violent assault of snapping, tearing, slicing and poking. This aggressive bug-type pokémon doesn't evolve into another form, so Pokémon Go trainers should feel free to power up this frightening-looking monster.

EXPERT ADVICE

Pinsir can be a common find in grassy places like public parks, fields and backyards. Even at a high CP, bug-type pokémon are known to be some of the weakest in a gym battle.

#128 TAUROS

CLASSIFICATION Wild Bull pokémon
TYPE Normal

Tauros, an intimidating, bullish pokémon with two horns and three tails, loves to work itself up into a frenzy. In Pokémon lore, it can be found in forests and charges anything that crosses its path. Tauros prefers to hang out in North America, meaning players there can take advantage of its powerful attacks, such as Earthquake.

EXPERT ADVICE

Tauros is quite common in North America, but if you live elsewhere, this pokémon can be a fairly difficult find. Fortunately, this "regional rare" can also be hatched from a 5km egg.

#129 MAGIKARP

CLASSIFICATION Fish pokémon
TYPE Water

The most humble of all pokémon, Magikarp is no doubt a familiar (if not altogether welcome) sight for anyone who has logged in time to Pokémon Go. The fish pokémon's primary purpose is to evolve into the fearsome Gyarados, but until then it remains as a slightly distressed-looking addition to the pokédex.

EXPERT ADVICE

Magikarp is absolutely useless in a gym battle. It has some of the lowest CP, attack, defense and stamina stats in the game. Its primary quick attack, Splash, doles out zero damage.

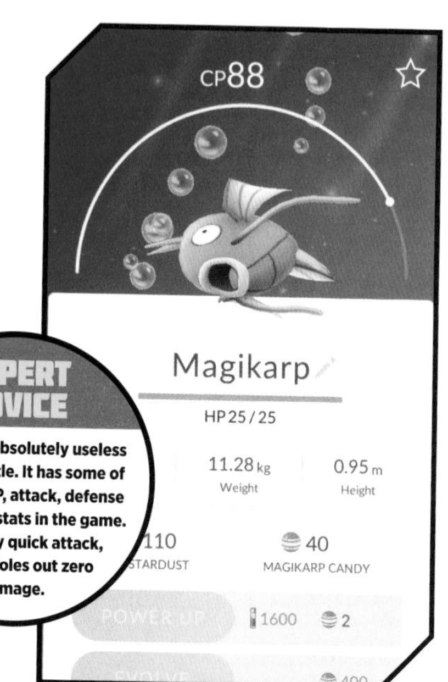

#130 GYARADOS

CLASSIFICATION Atrocious pokémon
TYPE Water/Flying

After stuffing it with 400 candies, the lowly Magikarp evolves into Gyarados, one of the most powerful Pokémon in the game. This sea dragon can unleash special moves such as Dragon Pulse and Hydro Pump in gym battles, making it a terrifying enemy, reliable ally and a badge of honor for the hardworking trainer.

EXPERT ADVICE

Gyarados, the epic water dragon, is worth fishing for the more than 100 Magikarps you'll have to catch to evolve him. It is one of the most powerful fighters in the Pokémon Go universe.

#131 LAPRAS

CLASSIFICATION Transport pokémon
TYPE Water/Ice

Resembling an ancient Plesiosaur and putting some trainers in mind of the legendary Loch Ness monster, Lapras is, according to Pokémon lore, a gentle giant that enjoys ferrying people across water. Its ice-type attacks, which include Frost Breath and Ice Shard, make it a good choice when facing a dragon-type pokémon.

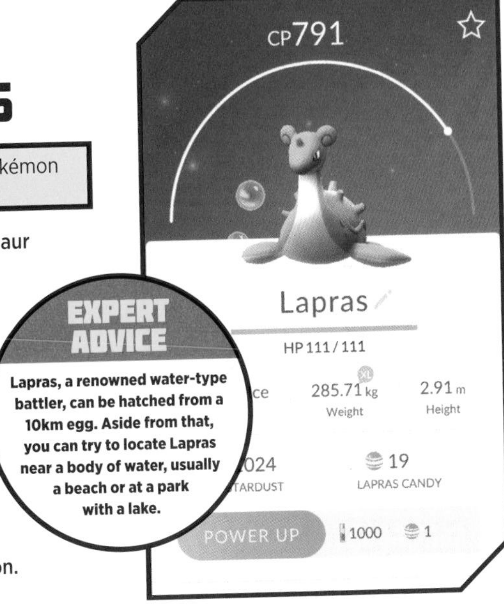

EXPERT ADVICE

Lapras, a renowned water-type battler, can be hatched from a 10km egg. Aside from that, you can try to locate Lapras near a body of water, usually a beach or at a park with a lake.

#132 DITTO

CLASSIFICATION Transform pokémon
TYPE Normal

Something of an enigma in Pokémon lore, Ditto can reproduce with almost any other pokémon to create eggs for that species, making it valuable in keeping endangered species alive. In the previous Pokémon games involving breeding your own monsters, Ditto's ability to be paired with any pokémon was a useful trait that may be repeated in Pokémon Go, should the app give trainers the opportunity to play matchmaker with their roster at a later date. We'll just have to wait and see!

EXPERT ADVICE

At the time of writing, Ditto doesn't appear to be out in the real world yet, but it is listed in the pokédex, so we know at some point in the future, it will make a possibly disguised entrance into the game.

#133 EEVEE

CLASSIFICATION Evolution pokémon
TYPE Normal

Believed in the Pokémon universe to possess a unique genetic structure that allows it to adapt perfectly to any given environment, Eevee is known as an evolution pokémon because the tiny quadruped can become one of three different evolved pokémon after 25 Eevee candies: Vaporeon, Jolteon or Flareon.

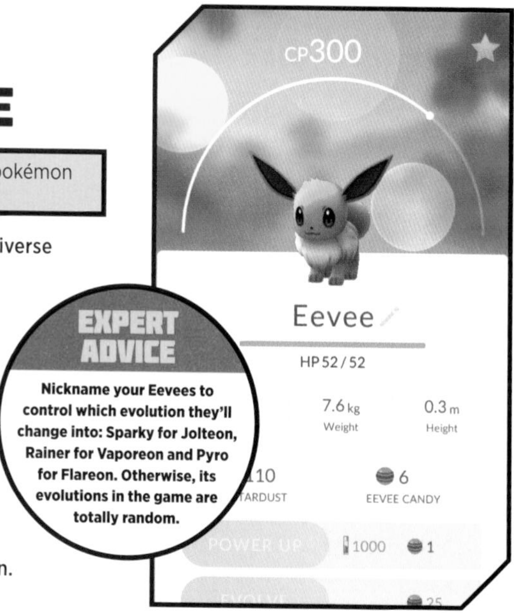

EXPERT ADVICE

Nickname your Eevees to control which evolution they'll change into: Sparky for Jolteon, Rainer for Vaporeon and Pyro for Flareon. Otherwise, its evolutions in the game are totally random.

#134 VAPOREON

CLASSIFICATION Bubble Jet pokémon
TYPE Water

EXPERT ADVICE

Vaporeon can stock a solid cache of water-type attacks, including Water Gun, Aqua Tail, Hydropump and Water Pulse. Its moves are super effective against fire-, rock- and ground-type pokémon.

One of the pokémon Eevee could choose to evolve into, Vaporeon, has a mermaid-like tail and gills in addition to its back legs. Although Vaporeon is not quite the powerhouse it was from the game's early days, this pokémon is still a solid choice for any trainer hoping to control their neighborhood gym.

#135 JOLTEON

CLASSIFICATION Lightning pokémon
TYPE Electric

Positively crackling with electricity, Jolteon is one of the possible evolved forms of Eevee. As befits its shocking nature, Jolteon assaults opponents with a variety of electric-based attacks, including Discharge, Thunder and Thunderbolt, which are especially damaging to water-type pokémon.

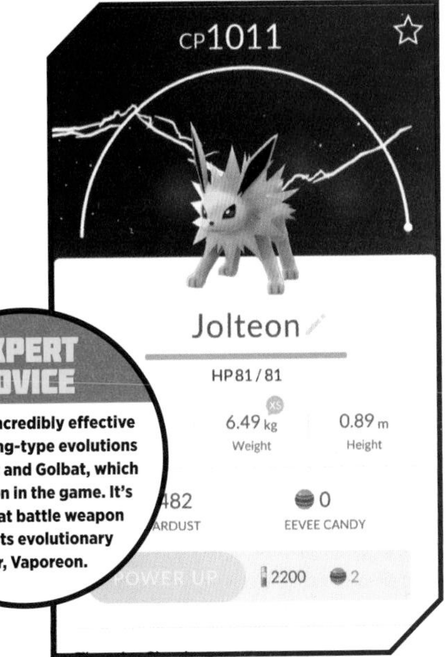

EXPERT ADVICE

Jolteon is incredibly effective against flying-type evolutions like Pidgeot and Golbat, which are common in the game. It's also a great battle weapon against its evolutionary sister, Vaporeon.

#136 FLAREON

CLASSIFICATION Flame pokémon
TYPE Fire

When Eevee evolves, it can become Flareon, a slightly larger, reddish-brown mammalian quadruped with fluffy tufts of yellow fur. Pokémon lore states Flareon's main weapon is a sac in which it can store and heat air, making it a literal fire-breather. Hence, its attacks are all fire type, including Heat Wave, Fire Blast and Flamethrower.

EXPERT ADVICE

Flareon is now the strongest Eevee evolution when it comes to hidden battle stats in the game. However, as a fire type, it is incredibly weak against Vaporeon, so be careful pitting it against its water-type equivalent in battle.

#137 PORYGON

CLASSIFICATION Virtual pokémon
TYPE Normal

Maybe the most meta of all pokémon, Porygon is made up entirely of programming code according to Pokémon lore, (as opposed to the "real life" flesh and blood pokémon). As a normal-type pokémon, none of its attacks are super effective in battle, but the rarity and strangeness of Porygon makes it a keeper for trainers.

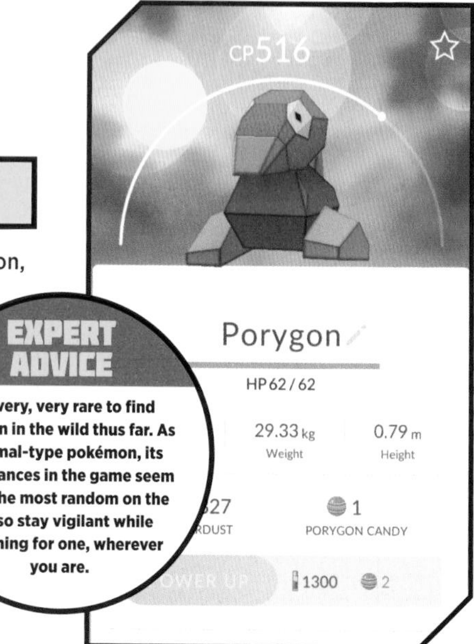

EXPERT ADVICE

It is very, very rare to find Porygon in the wild thus far. As a normal-type pokémon, its appearances in the game seem to be the most random on the list, so stay vigilant while searching for one, wherever you are.

#138 OMANYTE

CLASSIFICATION Spiral pokémon
TYPE Rock/Water

A small water-type (and in Pokémon lore, water-dwelling) pokémon, Omanyte resembles a cute sea slug. Being a rock and water-type pokémon, Omanyte's options of special moves reflect its mixed heritage. Ancient Power and Rock Tomb are both rock attacks, while Brine is a water-type attack.

EXPERT ADVICE

Like most fossil-like pokémon, Omanyte is a rare find in the wild. Search for it near marinas, at beaches or other places where water is present. It can also be hatched from a 10km egg.

#139 OMASTAR

CLASSIFICATION Spiral pokémon
TYPE Rock/Water

After 50 Omanyte candies, the little Omanyte becomes the beaked and dangerous Omastar. In the Pokémon world, this terrifying creature is able to use that clamp of a beak in order to hold so tight it can suck the insides right out of its prey. In Pokémon Go, it's an effective monster to keep with you.

EXPERT ADVICE

Make sure you're keeping your stock of pokéballs high when you're on the hunt for a rare pokémon like Omastar. It may take several attempts to capture this mysterious water type.

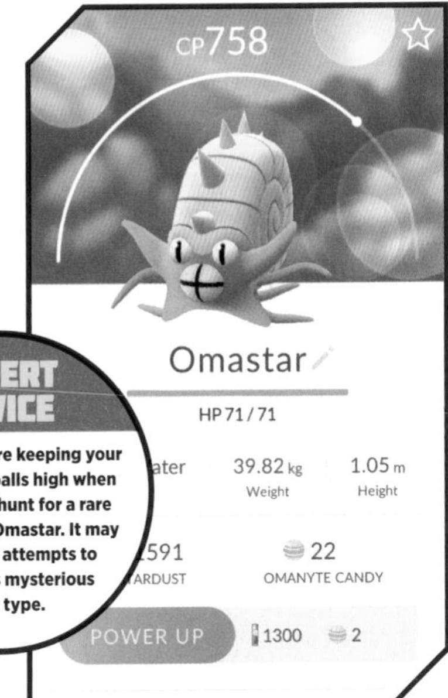

#140 KABUTO

CLASSIFICATION Shellfish pokémon
TYPE Rock/Water

A tiny pokémon with a large brown shell covering a body that would otherwise be exposed to attacks, Kabuto is the consummate water and rock-type pokémon, embodying the traits of both. Pokémon lore states Kabuto is an ancient pokémon that was believed to be extinct for 300 million years, but Pokémon Go trainers are able to find them in the wild.

EXPERT ADVICE

Kabuto is one of those rarities in the wild that can still be found by lucky low-level trainers. If water pokémon like Kabuto are not common in your area, know it can also be hatched from a 10km egg.

#141 KABUTOPS

CLASSIFICATION Shellfish pokémon
TYPE Rock/Water

After Kabuto is able to collect 50 of its candies, it evolves into Kabutops, which has a body that resembles an exoskeleton with intimidating bladed arms. A solid rock-type pokémon for any trainer looking to fill out his or her collection, Kabutops helps round out lineups for gym battles and is effective against other types such as bug and fire.

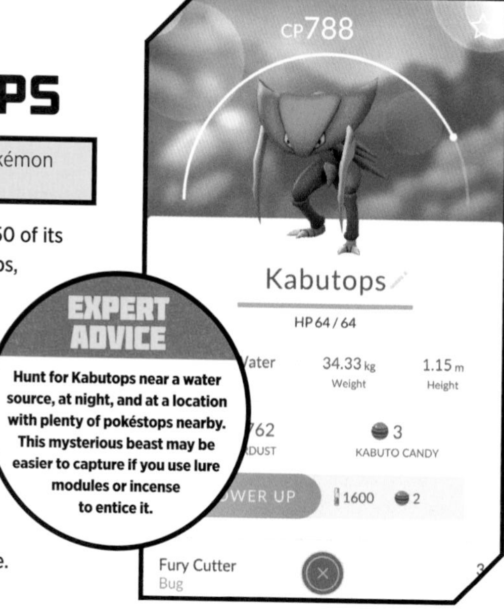

EXPERT ADVICE

Hunt for Kabutops near a water source, at night, and at a location with plenty of pokéstops nearby. This mysterious beast may be easier to capture if you use lure modules or incense to entice it.

#142 AERODACTYL

CLASSIFICATION Fossil pokémon
TYPE Rock

These dinosaur-like pokémon are extremely rare finds in the world of the Pokémon games. Fortunately for trainers in Pokémon Go, Aerodactyl appears to be more prevalent in the real world (or at least the world of Pokémon Go), meaning players can avail themselves of its huge muscular wings and powerful jaw in gym battles.

EXPERT ADVICE

According to player reports, Aerodactyl can be found anywhere in the world and is often discovered in backyards, parks and other outdoor spaces. You can also hatch Aerodactyl from a 10km egg.

#143 SNORLAX

CLASSIFICATION Sleeping pokémon
TYPE Normal

Snorlax is a bipedal pokémon with a large belly, two pointed teeth and claws on its hands and feet. It is also one of the best pokémon to bring with you in a gym battle (or to leave at a gym as a defender), thanks to its robust species stats. Just don't expect to stumble across one in the wild anytime soon—they are extremely rare finds for players.

EXPERT ADVICE

A level 1000+ Snorlax can be hatched from a 10km egg, even by low-level trainers. Its giant size, massive HP and sturdy stamina is incredibly useful in gym battles, so this one's worth walking for.

#144 ARTICUNO

CLASSIFICATION Freeze pokémon
TYPE Ice/Flying

With its majestic blue plumage and enormous wingspan, Articuno is one of the most beautiful sights in the entire world of the Pokémon games. But it's also one that hasn't yet graced Pokémon Go screens. Hopefully Niantic doesn't hew too closely to Pokémon lore and make the legendary bird pokémon obtainable only by climbing to the peak of a mountain. But given the pokémon's extreme power in the Game Boy games, it might just be worth such a trek.

EXPERT ADVICE

Articuno is one of three legendary birds in Pokémon Go that the game's team names are based on. Articuno is the mascot of Team Mystic. Players with a Dratini, a Dragonair or a Dragonite will unlock the legendary bird trio in their pokédex, giving these players the hint that the hard-to catch creatures are now open in the game and waiting to be caught.

#145 ZAPDOS

CLASSIFICATION Electric pokémon
TYPE Electric/Flying

In the Pokémon universe, Zapdos is one of the three legendary bird pokémon and, as you might expect from such a title, both extraordinarily rare and unbelievably powerful. The game's lore states that they live up in the thunderclouds and often cause storms to occur by flapping their wings. While trainers have yet to find this bird pokémon, whether on the ground or in the air, its power and utility in previous games in the Pokémon franchise indicate it will be more than worth the wait. This legendary pokémon's primary power in other games is Pressure, which decreases Zapdos's opponent's energy and makes it more difficult for their foe to attack.

EXPERT ADVICE

Zapdos is the official mascot for Team Instinct. Despite several hoax attempts, it appears legendary pokémon like Zapdos (along with Mew, Mewtwo, Articuno and Moltres) haven't yet appeared in the game, but we're awaiting special cheats and hacks to make them appear.

#146 MOLTRES

CLASSIFICATION Flame pokémon
TYPE Fire/Flying

Pokémon lore identifies Moltres as an extremely rare fire pokémon that shares many traits with the Phoenix of mythology in the real world, most importantly the ability to heal itself via unorthodox means. Both the Phoenix and Moltres regenerate their vitality by drawing upon the power of fire, in Moltres's case diving into the magma of an active volcano. Each time it flaps its massive wings, live embers produce bright flames that trail behind it. The bird has yet to make an appearance in Pokémon Go, and players shouldn't hang around active volcanoes in their search for the legendary pokémon. It's more likely Niantic will reveal the pokémon in a dramatic fashion.

EXPERT ADVICE

Moltres is the official team mascot of Team Valor. However, whether choosing team red will make you more likely to capture this legendary bird still has yet to be determined.

#147 DRATINI

CLASSIFICATION Dragon pokémon
TYPE Dragon

Dratini is the relatively small first stage pokémon that eventually becomes the formidable Dragonite. These weak pokémon may score major adorability points, but they probably won't be able to hold their own against higher-level pokémon in gym battles.

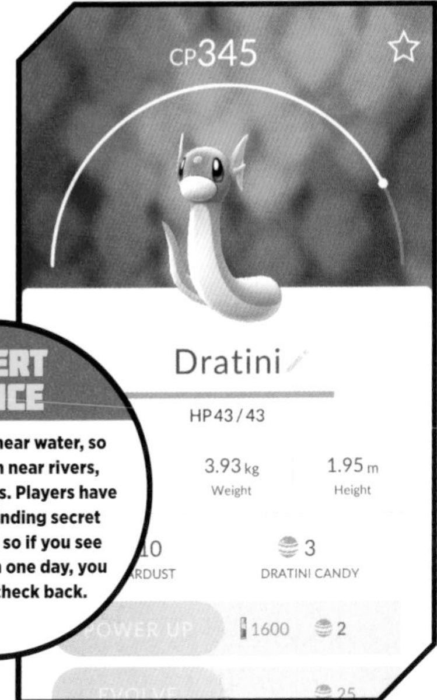

EXPERT ADVICE

Dratinis spawn near water, so search for them near rivers, lakes and beaches. Players have also reported finding secret Dratini "nests," so if you see one in a location one day, you may want to check back.

#148 DRAGONAIR

CLASSIFICATION Dragon pokémon
TYPE Dragon

The backstory of this pokémon tells us the three crystal orbs that embellish in Dragonair's skin help give it such powerful abilities. Whatever the source of its energy, this pokémon can be counted on to take on other dragon-type pokémon during gym battles. But unless you happen upon one in the wild, you'll have to amass 100 Dratini candies to evolve that lowly pokémon into Dragonair.

EXPERT ADVICE

Dragonair can be found fully evolved in the wild, most commonly near water. Dragon types are only super effective against other dragon-type pokémon, so be careful battling with it.

EXPERT ADVICE

Dragonites hatched or discovered out in the wild will have one of a wide array of special attacks, including Aqua Tail, Dragon Claw, Fire Punch, Hyper Beam, Slam and Twister.

#149 DRAGONITE

CLASSIFICATION Dragon pokémon
TYPE Dragon/Flying

Dratini eventually evolves to its ultimate form Dragonite, which looks a bit like a friendlier version of Charizard, but its mystical abilities make it formidable against almost any pokémon. A great addition to any trainer's collection (especially if they are gearing up for some gym battles), Dragonite is a sign that you've made it to the top echelons in the Pokémon Go universe.

#150 MEWTWO

CLASSIFICATION Genetic pokémon
TYPE Psychic

According to Pokémon lore, Mewtwo is a unique monster created by a team of scientists, rather than a creature that naturally evolved over time. By manipulating the genes of a Mew, science gave birth to one of the most powerful pokémon in existence, capable of telepathy, telekinesis and mind control.

Its elaborate backstory is reflected in its stats, which are the most impressive out of all the pokémon we know about in Pokémon Go. However, no trainer has yet to find and catch a Mewtwo, though speculation abounds that it will become available via a special event. Let's hope it happens soon and that you are one of the lucky first to catch Mewtwo!

EXPERT ADVICE

Nobody knows how Mewtwo will finally reveal itself in Pokémon Go, but a trailer for the app teased a possible scenario where trainers will work together on a huge scale to nab it.

#151 MEW

CLASSIFICATION New Species pokémon
TYPE Psychic

When the original "Red" and "Blue" games reached the United States, the pokémon Mew found itself the subject of some of the most compelling and stubborn rumors in video game history. As sworn by legions of players and told on playgrounds across the country, the truck near the S.S. *Anne* could somehow be moved, revealing a pokéball with a Mew inside. While that rumor was decidely false, it proves how sought-after this pokémon can be. Although Mew (like its meaner relative Mewtwo) has yet to make an appearence, you can be certain the first trainer who finds one will shout it from the rooftops.

EXPERT ADVICE

If the original *Pokémon* movie is any clue, Mew should be able to defeat Mewtwo in a fairly matched battle. However, the game's "secret stats" don't bode well for the pink guy.

Pokémon Go has inspired trainers to explore their neighborhoods in search of pokémon, as these players are doing, Tokyo, Japan.

EXPERT ADVICE

If you're having a hard time aiming at pokémon when you're trying to catch them, turn off AR mode. This will automatically center the pokémon on your phone screen and eliminate distracting movement from the background.

TRACK 'EM DOWN

Sick of walking around in circles in a frustrated pursuit of that Pidgeotto? We're here to help.

Stripped of all the battles and strategy about maximizing CP, taking over gyms and mastering the theory of evolution, Pokémon Go offers trainers a simple, undeniable pleasure—finding and catching pokémon. But actually tracking down the most desirable pokémon involves more than just wandering around your neighborhood with your phone outstretched hoping to find a Squirtle in a sea of Staryus. To build an awe-inspiring collection of pokémon, you need to get wise to the ins and outs of how, why and (most importantly) where the little critters spawn. Read up, and start hunting with a purpose.

FOLLOW THE SIGNS

Perhaps preferring to preserve the mystery of the original Pokémon Game Boy games, Pokémon Go eschews providing a detailed map of where most of the pokémon surrounding you are. Clicking the bar filled with pokémon icons on the bottom right corner of the screen brings up another screen showing pokémon in your general vicinity. How far away are they? No one really knows, especially since Niantic has removed its rudimentary "footsteps" tracking icons from the game and shut down all outside tracking apps for the time being. This makes tracking pokémon more of an art than a science. However, trainers have sussed out some basic rules to help get in range of that Onix.

The pokémon closest to the top left corner is the one nearest to you. If you leave the "nearby pokémon" screen on, walk in one direction, and if you see a pokémon move closer to the top left corner, that means you are heading in the right direction. Once you've closed the distance between you and the pokémon enough to move it up your list, you should be able to find it without too much trouble. Once you're 70 meters away from a pokémon, it will pop up on your map.

While everyone's figured out certain types of pokémon appear more in certain real-world environments (see the chart on page 154 for details), the same seems to hold true on the micro level—individual pokémon sometimes reliably respawn in the same exact location. If you keep finding that Sandshrew in the alley by your office during your lunch break, check again when you leave to go home—there's a chance it will have respawned, and you've discovered a rock-solid method for farming multiple copies of a certain pokémon.

HUNT IN PACKS

Niantic, the company behind Pokémon Go, doesn't assign the locations for every Hitmonchan and Snorlax randomly. Diligent trainers have determined pokémon tend to spawn in areas with the highest amount of cellular activity—meaning places where people check their phones often. So while Ash, Brock and Misty would often head out into the hinterlands to find

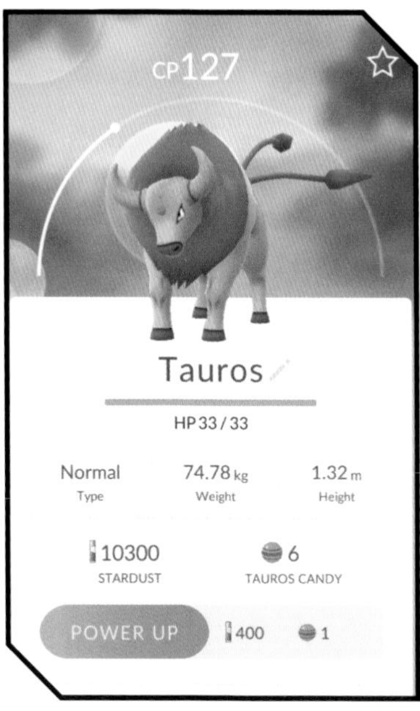

pokémon, you should start hanging around banks, stores, restaurants and other heavily trafficked areas (without making a nuisance of yourself).

LOCAL FAVORITES

Another thing to keep in mind is the availability of pokémon varies not just from environment to environment, but also continent to continent. Fortunately for trainers wanting to collect most of the game's pokémon without applying for a passport, the number of region-exclusive pokémon is limited to four: Mr. Mime performs in Europe, Tauros stampedes through North America, Farfetch'd is most prevalent in Asia and Kangaskhan makes its home in Australia. But don't worry if you haven't got frequent flier miles. You can also hatch them from eggs.

EXPERT ADVICE

Above all other facets of the game, level reigns supreme. The higher the level, the better the items, the rarer the pokémon and the stronger the monsters you will attract. So start leveling up!

FAVORITE HANG OUTS

Looking for specific pokémon types? This chart reveals where you should hunt to catch every one in the game.

Pokémon trainers who are part of the online community The Silph Road have spent countless hours researching the probability of a pokémon spawning being a certain type based on the real-world environment in which it spawns. For example, if you are in a residential area, there's a 37 percent chance that a spawning pokémon will be a normal type. Like most things in Pokémon Go, these percentages are a work in progress, but this should at least point you in the right direction!

EXPERT ADVICE

Wondering where in the heck your neighbor found enough Dratinis in the desert to evolve his Dragonair? Ask him. Players are constantly stumbling upon hidden "nests" where certain types of pokémon repeatedly spawn, even if they're technically uncommon in your area. A degree of randomness is purposely built into the game.

POKÉMON TYPE

ENVIRONMENT	NORMAL	BUG	POISON	WATER	FIRE
WETLAND	9%	3%	3%	61%	12%
RIVERBANK	8%	4%	1%	76%	2%
LAKE	25%	25%	15%	35%	0%
SALTWATER BEACH	4%	7%	7%	50%	7%
FARMLAND	29%	14%	0%	0%	14%
UNIVERSITY	41%	12%	9%	13%	2%
GOLF COURSE	6%	0%	6%	6%	6%
PARK	18%	8%	8%	31%	8%
PARKING LOT	43%	15%	8%	7%	6%
INDUSTRIAL	30%	22%	11%	11%	7%
RESIDENTIAL	37%	16%	12%	5%	5%
MEADOW	53%	19%	5%	8%	1%

	POKÉMON TYPE				
ENVIRONMENT	GROUND	GRASS	FIGHTING	ROCK	FAIRY
WETLAND	0%	0%	0%	6%	0%
RIVERBANK	0%	3%	0%	0%	2%
LAKE	0%	0%	0%	0%	0%
SALTWATER BEACH	0%	11%	0%	4%	11%
FARMLAND	14%	0%	0%	29%	0%
UNIVERSITY	3%	3%	2%	2%	0%
GOLF COURSE	12%	41%	6%	6%	0%
PARK	6%	4%	4%	4%	1%
PARKING LOT	4%	5%	3%	3%	1%
INDUSTRIAL	2%	6%	1%	4%	3%
RESIDENTIAL	7%	5%	3%	3%	2%
MEADOW	1%	8%	0%	1%	1%

	POKÉMON TYPE				
ENVIRONMENT	ELECTRIC	PSYCHIC	DRAGON	ICE	GHOST*
WETLAND	6%	0%	0%	0%	??%
RIVERBANK	0%	0%	5%	0%	??%
LAKE	0%	0%	0%	0%	??%
SALTWATER BEACH	0%	0%	0%	0%	??%
FARMLAND	0%	0%	0%	0%	??%
UNIVERSITY	10%	2%	0%	1%	??%
GOLF COURSE	2%	0%	12%	0%	??%
PARK	2%	1%	1%	1%	??%
PARKING LOT	3%	1%	0%	0%	??%
INDUSTRIAL	1%	1%	0%	0%	??%
RESIDENTIAL	2%	1%	0%	0%	??%
MEADOW	1%	0%	1%	1%	??%

*Although no ghost types were reported in the data for this study, they obviously exist.

THEORY OF EVOLUTION

The ins and outs of developing your pokémon for maximum efficiency.

The first thing you need to learn about evolving your pokémon is that it takes candies. Lots of candies. You'll earn three candies per pokémon you capture in the wild, and one candy for every pokémon you transfer back to Professor Willow. You can also get any number of candies from hatching eggs. Candies are specific to each type of pokémon and cannot be transferred to different species to evolve, unless it's related in its evolutionary history. So, you can feed a Kakuna some Weedle candies to turn it into a Beedrill, but your Charmander will not take the same snack as your Bulbasaur to help it transform into Charmeleon.

EXPERT ADVICE

In addition to aiding in evolution, candies help you power-up your pokémon, raising both their CP and HP scores. So even if your Pidgey has reached its final form, Pidgeot, you're still going to want to catch some Pidgeys to help give it a battle boost later on. Pokémon require different amounts of candy and stardust to power them up.

Just as viewers of the anime and players of the original games will remember, in Pokémon Go the moment of evolution is a milestone event and is heavily produced.

Magikarp might not be too useful—just look at it on its side like that—but once it evolves, the difference is as stark as the difference between a fish and a sea dragon.

Each pokémon also requires a slightly different number of candies to evolve. For instance, Rattata and Eevee only need 25 candies to evolve to their next stage, but to evolve your Magikarp into the mighty dragon pokémon Gyarados, you'll need to stock up a full 400 candies (catching at least 100 Magikarp) while you're out and about playing the game. Essentially, that means you should be catching as many pokémon as possible out in the wild, even if you've already added them to your pokédex. Cashing in those duplicates for candies will help you to evolve your pokémon later on. Generally, the more candies it takes to power up a pokémon, the more powerful its evolution will be (with notable exceptions like Eevee, which can evolve into the battle-ready Jolteon, Flareon or Vaporeon after relatively little effort).

To evolve a pokémon, head to its profile page and simply hit the green "evolve" button located directly underneath the green "power up button" under its photo. If you don't have enough candies to evolve your pokémon just yet, the button will be faded out and won't allow you to press it, so it should be pretty clear when your pokémon is ready to take the next step in its evolutionary history. You can evolve your pokémon anytime during the game (except when it's stationed in a gym) as long as you have enough species-specific candies in your bag to do so. But don't feel the need to evolve your pokémon as soon as you are able—there are some strategies you may want to keep in mind to get the most success from those sweets.

First things first: Trainer level is the top stat in Pokémon Go and affects the CP of every pokémon you see out in the wild. Your best bet for getting a high-level evolution is to only evolve your pokémon with the highest-possible CP scores. So maybe don't power up any pokémon while you're still a low-level

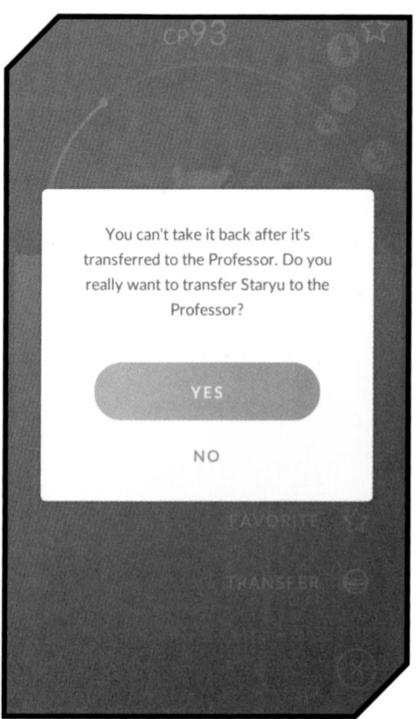

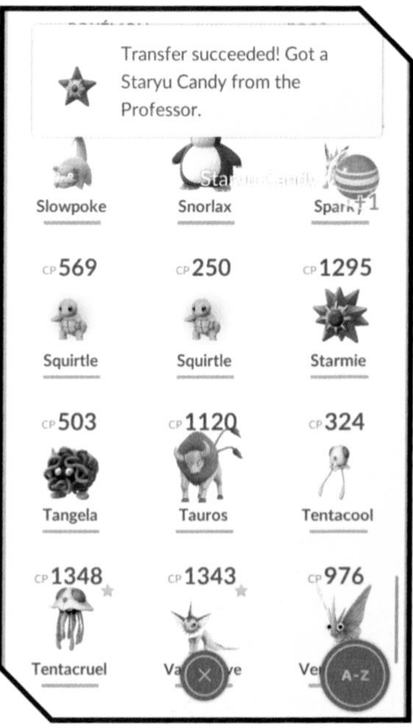

Pokémon designated as a favorite have a gold star in their profile (as Tentacruel and Vaporeon do in the screen above and to the right) and are impossible to accidentally transfer to Professor Willow.

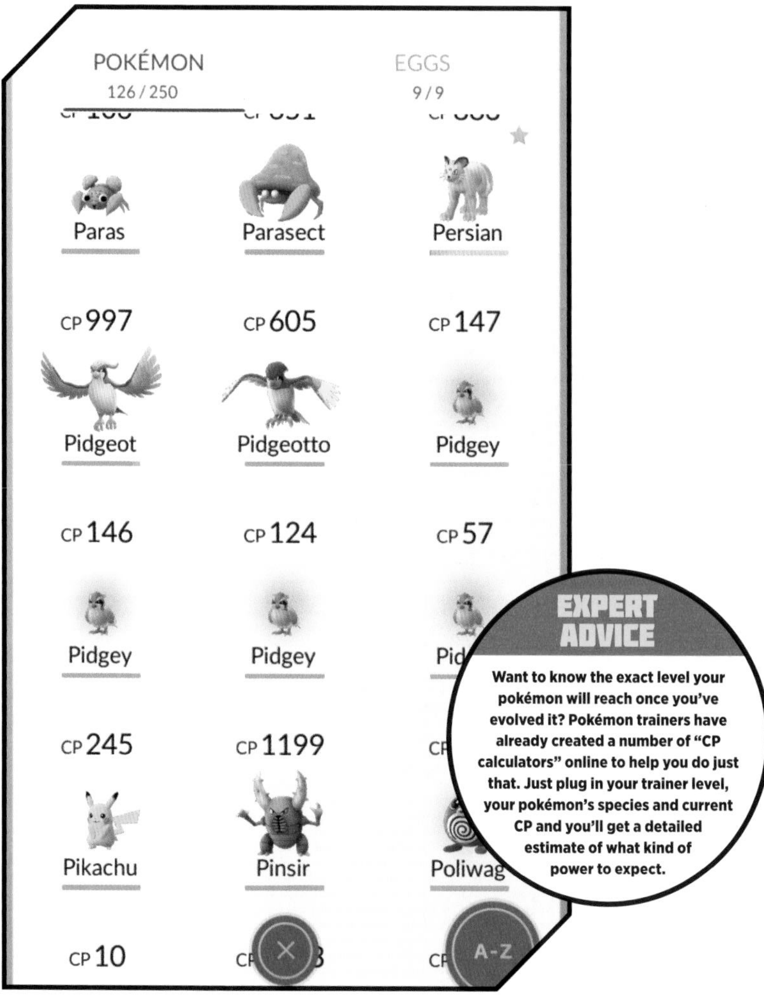

EXPERT ADVICE

Want to know the exact level your pokémon will reach once you've evolved it? Pokémon trainers have already created a number of "CP calculators" online to help you do just that. Just plug in your trainer level, your pokémon's species and current CP and you'll get a detailed estimate of what kind of power to expect.

trainer. Instead, just catch as many low-level critters as possible until you level up enough for the real strong beasts to come by.

Another thing to consider before evolving a pokémon is its CP progress on the arc behind its picture in your backpack. Ideally, you'll want to evolve a pokémon that has progressed about 80 to 90 percent of its individual CP cap. Should you use stardust to achieve that? Well, tons of players have tested powering up with stardust before evolving and evolving before powering

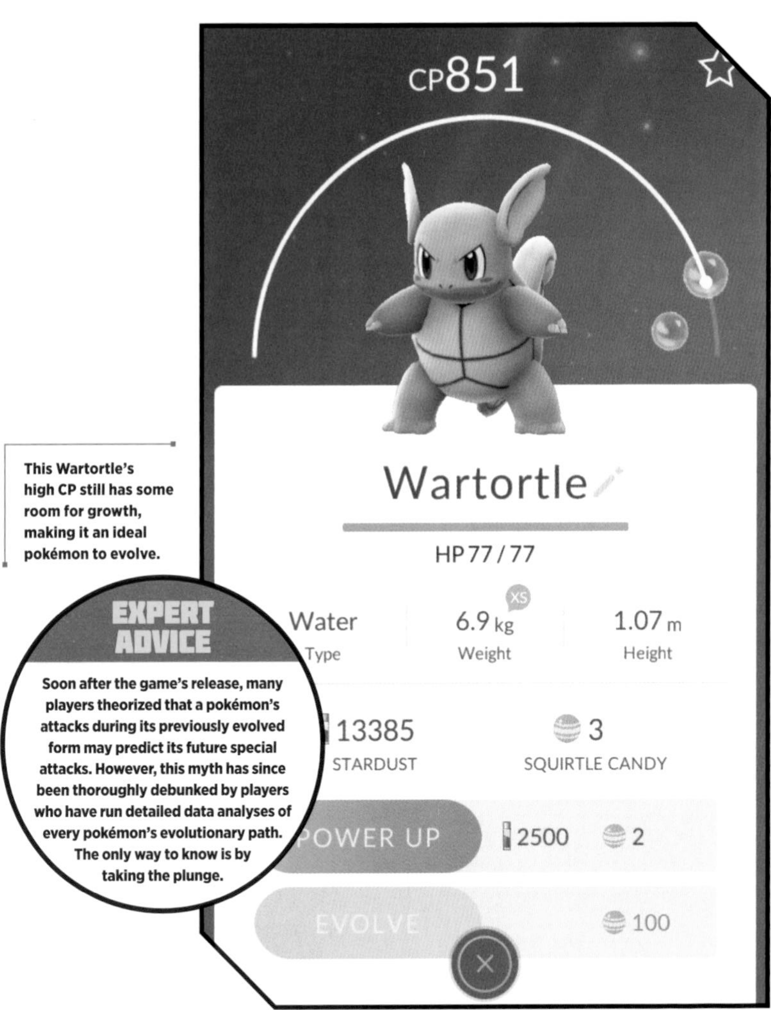

This Wartortle's high CP still has some room for growth, making it an ideal pokémon to evolve.

EXPERT ADVICE

Soon after the game's release, many players theorized that a pokémon's attacks during its previously evolved form may predict its future special attacks. However, this myth has since been thoroughly debunked by players who have run detailed data analyses of every pokémon's evolutionary path. The only way to know is by taking the plunge.

up, and it seems to make little difference in a pokémon's end CP result. It's really more a matter of your playing style. Do you want to go to battle right away at Level 5 with a super-strong Clefairy or would you prefer to keep it in your pocket for several days until you can save up enough candies to evolve the pink rotund pokémon into its stronger (though no less adorable) form, Clefable?

Another major thing to take into account is that there is no way to predict whether your pokémon's attack moves will change when it evolves. Some do,

Different pokémon of the same species can possess different moves, as seen with these Poliwags. You never know what moves an evolved pokémon will have until you take the plunge!

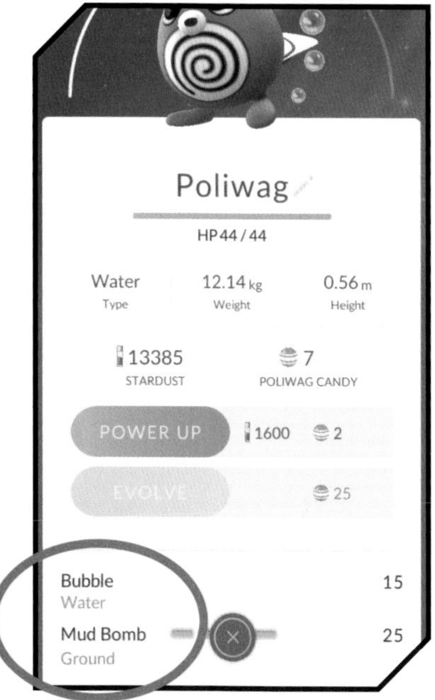

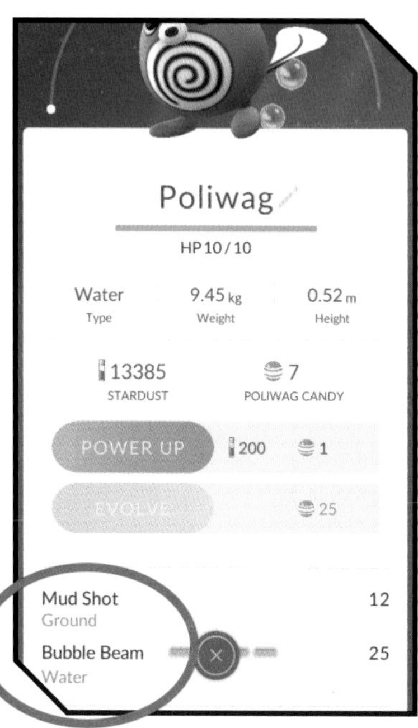

some don't. It's completely random. So it might be best to evolve your pokémon first then power up later, in case your pokémon evolves and gets stuck with a less-than-ideal skill set. Spending stardust and candies to power up a pokémon with a weak special attack is a waste of precious resources. Minding all of those considerations, our advice is to evolve first, then power up later once your pokémon have hit their fully evolved form.

Also know that evolving fully restores a pokémon's HP, so don't worry about healing a pokémon with a potion before you evolve it. Every evolution you achieve will also award you 500 XP. If you evolve a pokémon you haven't caught before you'll get an extra 500 XP bonus on top of that.

You also should use some strategy when dealing with pokémon that have three-stage evolutions. **Evolving to stage two as soon as you are able might not be your best bet for achieving a high CP pokémon. Instead, save up enough candies to do both final evolutions at once.** Why? Well, in all the time that you're collecting pokémon to cash in for candies to evolve it, you'll probably level up and start finding stronger copies of that pokémon. So waiting will allow you to power-up the strongest pokémon possible, and gain at least 1000 XP while doing so.

Let's look at an example of this: You have a 200 CP Nidoran, and finally get 25 candies to make it a 336 CP Nidorino

Saving up multiple versions of the same pokémon like Pidgey in the above example allows for better evolutionary possibilities, as well as for the possibility of a candy transfer (right).

that may someday, after 100 candies, turn into a 615 CP Nidoking. But in the time it takes you to capture enough pokémon to earn 100 candies for that Nidoking, you will probably have leveled up and found a much stronger 400 CP Nidoran, which could turn into an 672 CP Nidorino and therefore a 1230 CP Nidoking. A lot of players have learned

EXPERT ADVICE

As a rule of thumb, try not to evolve any pokémon that has a CP score lower than 500, if you want its final form to be packing a 1000+ battle advantage. This will ensure that every pokémon you spend your precious candy on will be able to at least hold its own against other trainers' pokémon at the gym. Turn all weak pokémon into Professor Willow.

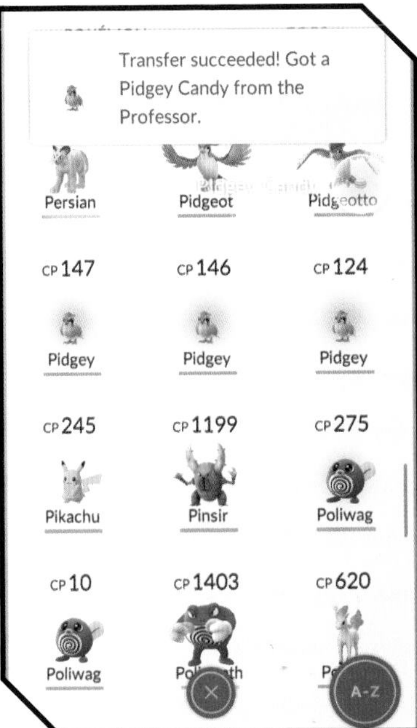

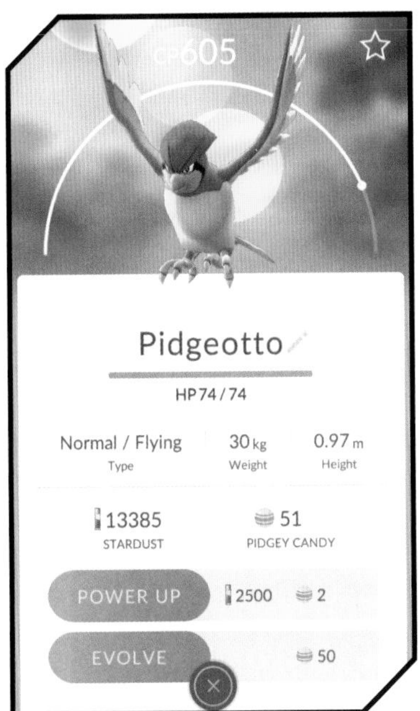

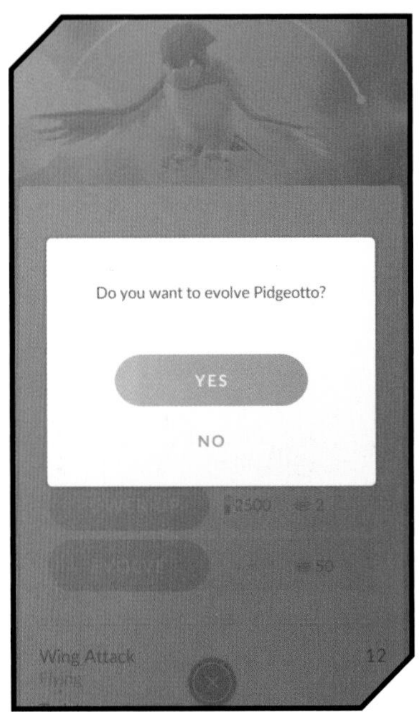

this lesson the hard way (while wasting a ton of candy in the process), so it's important to take note if you're looking for max evolutionary efficiency.

As a side note, you can also evolve weaker copies of a pokémon for a quick XP boost in the game. This is a trick called "farming" that lots of players use to help them level up quickly—yet another reason why it's important to catch every pokémon you see out in the wild, even if you already have it in your pokédex. For example, a trainer may collect 20 Pidgeys, turn all but two of them in to Professor Willow and then evolve the two into Pidgeottos purely for the level boost. Often, players will save up so much candy they can do multiple evolutions at once and activate a lucky egg while doing so to double that progress. Just know before you spend your candies that you probably aren't going to end up using your dozens of farmed

Since the beginning of the franchise, knowing how and when to evolve your pokémon has remained one of the skills separating newbies from the masters.

Pidgeottos in a battle, and because your pocket only holds 250 pokémon, you'll eventually end up turning them into the Professor. Pokémon farming is essentially a balancing act between how fast you want to advance in the game and how much organization and evolutions you want to keep track of.

All of that being said, saving up all your stardust and refusing to evolve or power up any pokémon until you're a Level 20 trainer wrangling in some of the strongest pokémon ever can get pretty boring. Balance your zeal for evolutionary efficiency with your idea of fun as a trainer. You can always find and evolve a stronger Eevee later on in the game and swap out your top battlers as you go. Sure, it's not technically the most efficient method for spending your candies and stardust, but it'll fill up your pokédex faster and make the whole journey a lot more enjoyable along the way.

JUST REWARDS

When you gain a level in Pokémon Go, you also gain free items. Take a look at what's in store for you as you rack up the levels.

LEVEL 2-3

10 Pokéballs

LEVEL 4

15 Pokéballs

EXPERT ADVICE

When flicking a pokéball at a creature you want to catch, imagine an underhanded throw or a three-pointer in basketball, not a fastball.

LEVEL 5

20 Pokéballs, 10 Potions,
10 Revives, 1 Incense

Unlocks: Gyms, Potions and Revives

LEVEL 6

15 Pokéballs, 10 Potions,
5 Revives, 1 Egg Incubator

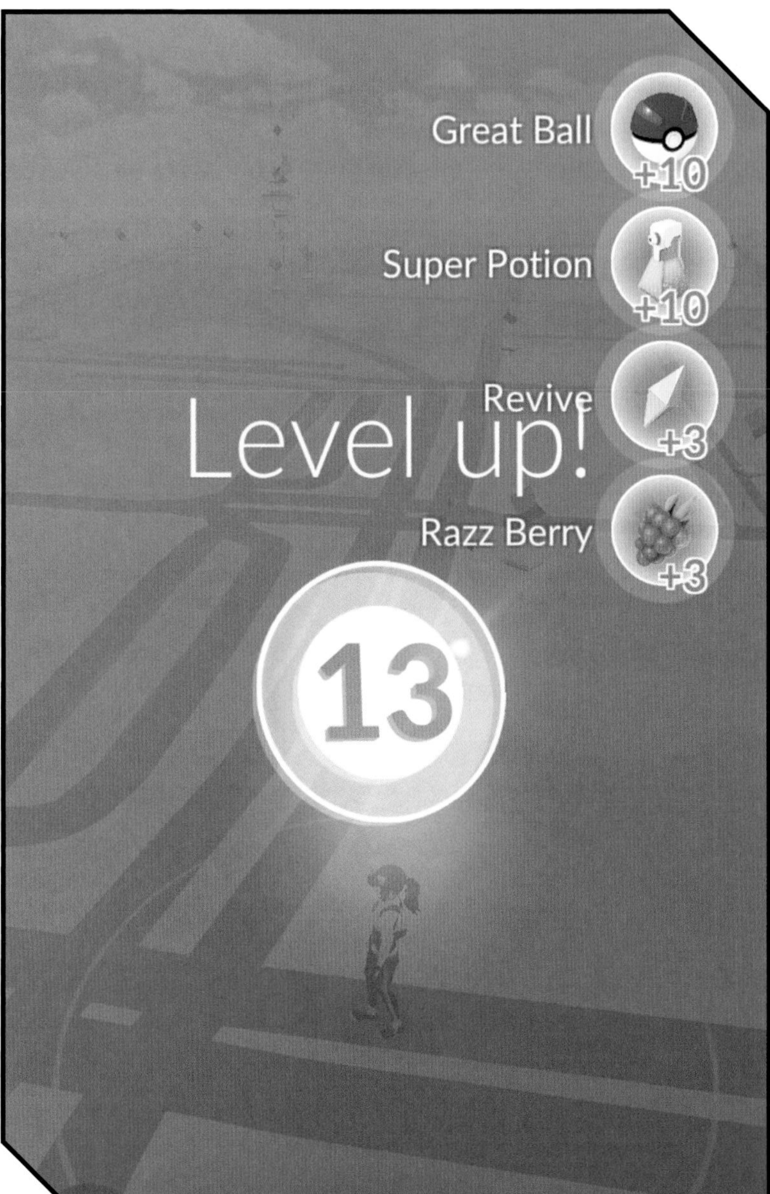
Great Ball
+10
Super Potion
+10
Revive
+3
Level up!
Razz Berry
+3
13

LEVEL 7

15 Pokéballs, 10 Potions, 5 Revives, 1 Incense

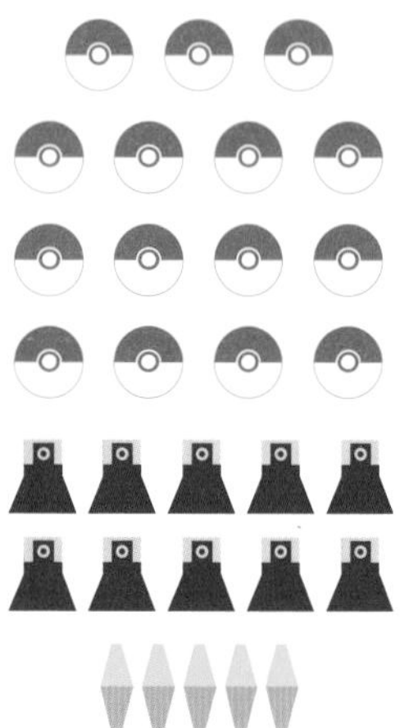

LEVEL 8

15 Pokéballs, 10 Potions, 5 Revives, 10 Razz Berries, 1 Lure Module.

Unlocks: Razz Berries

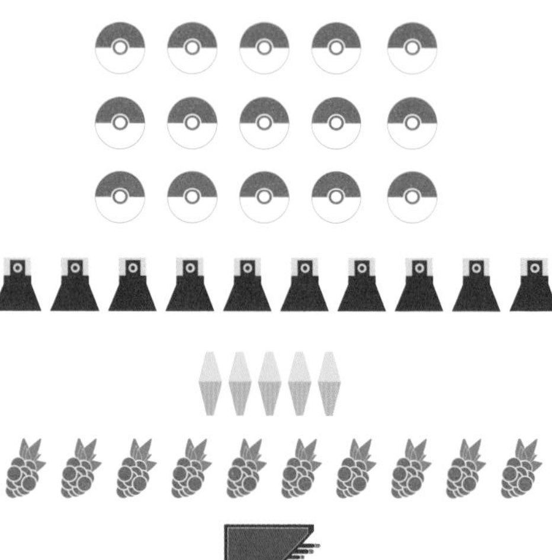

LEVEL 9

5 Pokéballs, 10 Potions, 5 Revives, 3 Razz Berries, 1 Lucky Egg

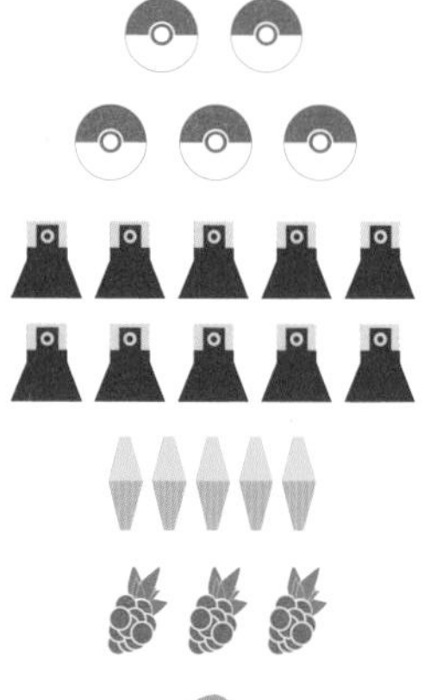

LEVEL 10

20 Pokéballs, 20 Super Potions, 10 Revives, 1 Razz Berry, 1 Incense, 1 Lucky Egg, 1 Egg Incubator

Unlocks: Super Potions

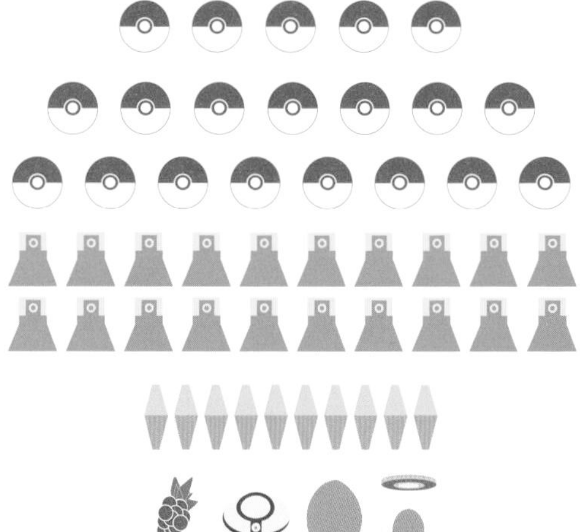

LEVEL 11

15 Pokéballs, 10 Super Potions, 3 Revives, 3 Razz Berries

LEVEL 12

20 Great Balls, 10 Super Potions, 3 Revives, 3 Razz Berries

Unlocks: Great Balls

LEVEL 13-14

10 Great Balls, 10 Super Potions, 3 Revives, 3 Razz Berries

EXPERT ADVICE

Razz Berries can raise your chances of catching a pokémon, but they also make ball tosses curve. Adjust your throw after using one.

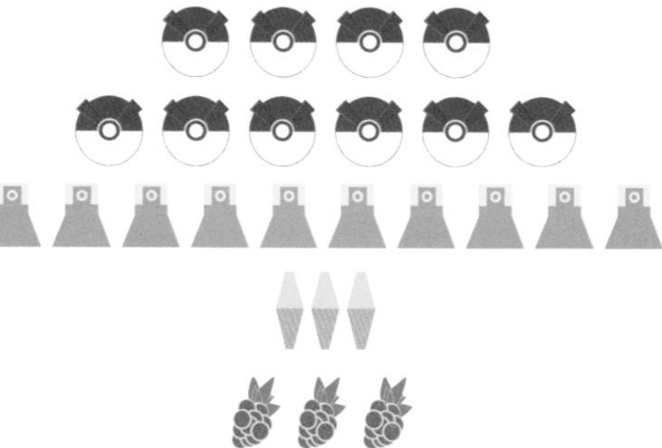

LEVEL 15

15 Great Balls, 20 Hyper Potions, 10 Revives, 10 Razz Berries, 1 Incense, 1 Lucky Egg, 1 Egg Incubator

Unlocks: Hyper Potions

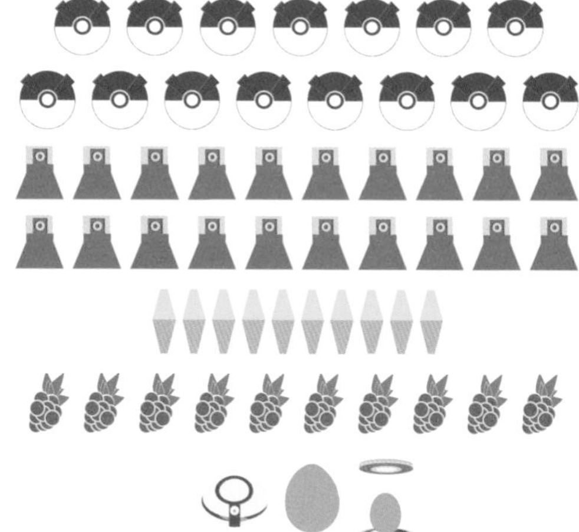

LEVEL 16-19

15 Great Balls, 10 Hyper Potions, 5 Revives, 5 Razz Berries

EXPERT ADVICE

Don't waste pokéballs or great balls on the evolved forms of common pokémon, especially if you already have one. You don't get any more stardust or candy for catching a Pidgeotto or Pidgeot than you do for a common Pidgey, and the latter are way easier to catch.

LEVEL 20

20 Ultra Balls, 20 Hyper Potions, 20 Revives, 20 Razz Berries, 2 Incense, 2 Lucky Eggs, 2 Egg Incubators, 2 Lure Modules **Unlocks: Ultra Balls**

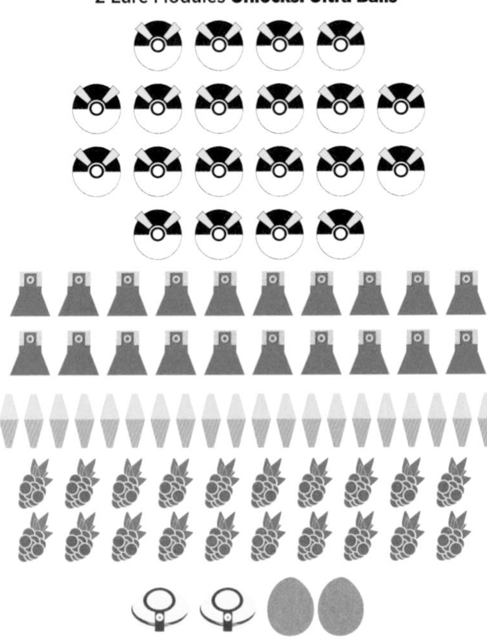

LEVEL 21-24

10 Ultra Balls, 10 Hyper Potions, 10 Revives, 10 Razz Berries

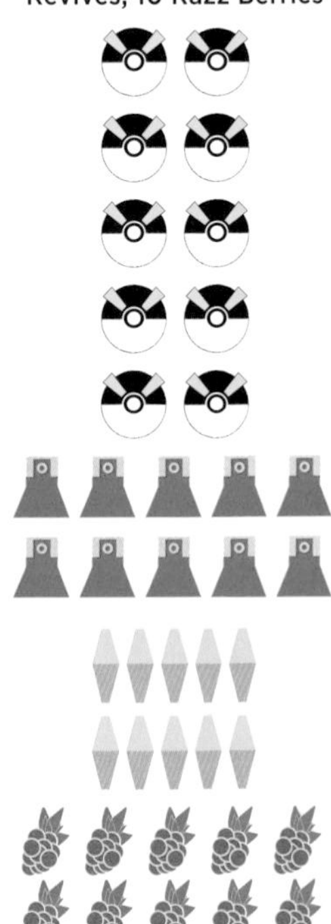

LEVEL 25

25 Ultra Balls, 20 Max Potions, 15 Revives, 15 Razz Berries, 1 Incense, 1 Lucky Egg, 1 Egg Incubator, 1 Lure Module **Unlocks: Max Potions**

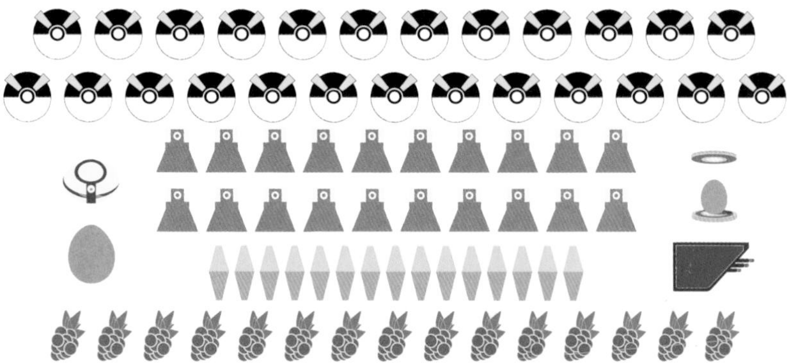

LEVEL 26-29

10 Ultra Balls, 15 Max Potions, 10 Revives, 15 Razz Berries

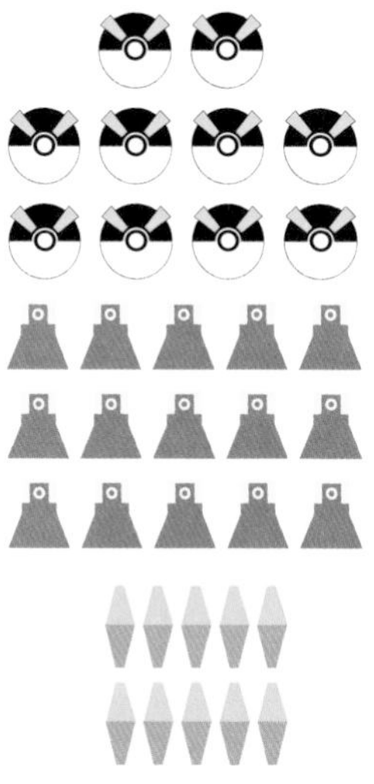

LEVEL 30

30 Ultra Balls, 20 Max Potions, 20 Max Revives, 20 Razz Berries, 3 Incense, 3 Lucky Eggs, 3 Egg Incubators, 3 Lure Modules **Unlocks: Max Revive**

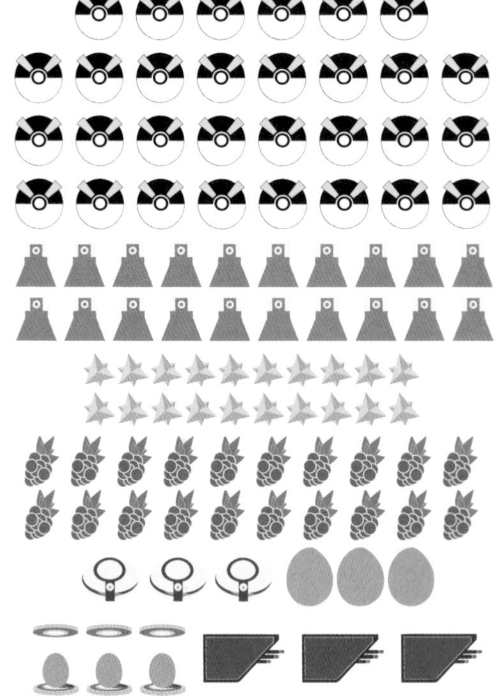

BATTLE TACTICS BREAKDOWN

Get the leg up on your rivals with these expert strategies on pokémon combat.

If you find a pokémon of yours going up against a more evolved version of the same species, don't despair right away. Use your regular strategy and look for clean hits to punch above your proverbial weight.

Currently, battles in Pokémon Go are limited to gyms, where teams work together to defend a location or topple a rival team's gym for their own. Unlike the original Pokémon games, you cannot individually battle other pokémon trainers or fight pokémon you find out in the wild, though some players theorize these parts of the game might be introduced by Niantic later on. In the meantime, prepare to spend way more time collecting pokémon and gathering items from pokéstops than you do at the gym. However, if you want to prove your trainer street cred and get into the spirit of competition with other players,

EXPERT ADVICE

All pokémon of the same species are not created equal. Attack speeds, HP scores and even heights and weights can differ drastically from pokémon to pokémon as well as the crucial CP stat, so you may want to look at more than that top number when determining which monsters will be your best fighter in a gym battle.

Pidgeys might be everywhere in Pokémon Go, but that doesn't mean they should be ignored. As the pokédex on the left shows, once enough Pidgeys are collected and evolve into Pidgeot, the flying pokémon can stand against far more fearsome beasts in terms of CP.

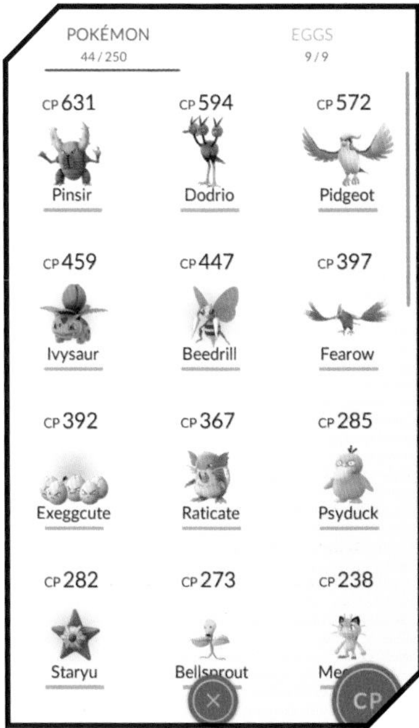

battling is one of the best ways to do so. **Plus, being in control of gyms is an awesome way to earn free coins in the pokéshop, which you can spend to buy item swag in the game.**

One of the most important facets of becoming a battle master happens before you ever step foot into a gym. Playing to win is all about preparation, which you do by catching a wide array of pokémon, evolving them and leveling them up with stardust to make sure your fighting roster can hold their own in a rumble.

Pokémon CP, or combat power, is arguably the most important measure of your pokémon's abilities at the gym. When you first encounter a pokémon in the wild, you will usually see its CP level floating above its head. If you see "???" instead, that probably means you are attempting to capture

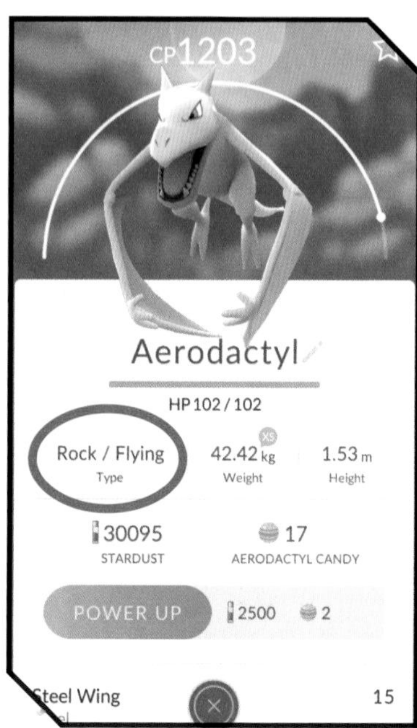

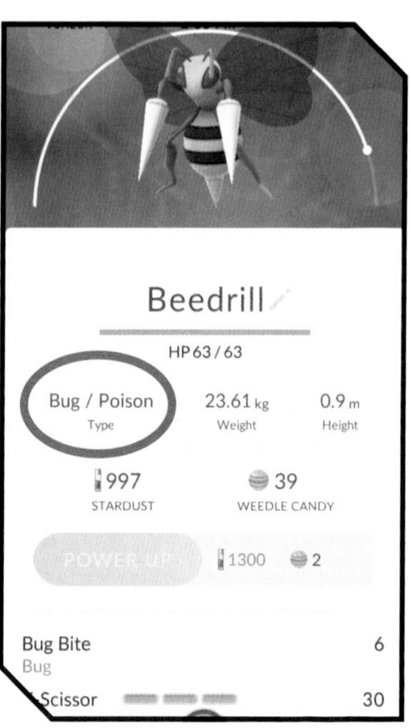

When choosing pokémon to battle, it helps to think logically, as though it were a game of rock-paper-scissors with plenty of extra options in play. Rock-type pokémon, for example, are fairly immune to poison.

a pokémon with a relatively high CP power, so break out those great balls if you've got them. **In general, pokémon with higher CP measures will defeat pokémon with lower CPs, especially if the disparity is large,** so you'll want to start preparing for a battle by making sure your pokémon have the highest CP you can muster.

Next, check out the attacks of every pokémon in your cache. Each monster will have two different moves: A quick attack and a special attack. Quick attacks can be repeated over and over again with little lag time and no need to "charge up." Special attacks deal much more damage than quick attacks, but take some time to build up before you can unleash them on an opponent. You'll see the number of damage each attack doles out next to its name on each pokémon's profile page. Every monster's moves will generally relate to its type, but not always, so make sure you're familiar with all of your pokémon's attacks before you enter into battle. To make things even more complicated, every pokémon will have a slightly different roster of moves, even if they are of the same species, so one Charmander you find out in the wild might have a Flame Blast attack, while another might be packing a more powerful Flamethrower up its sleeve. You'll want to pick the pokémon with both the highest CP and the strongest attacks to battle.

EXPERT ADVICE

Every time you capture or evolve a pokémon, the game "rolls" its stats, slightly changing all of the numbers that you'll find on its main profile page. There are charts online that list every pokémon's potential quick and special attack moves, which are worth checking out if you're looking to find monsters with max battle efficiency.

Though it evolves from the relatively docile Horsea, Seadra is covered with spiny quills and has a very touchy temper.

Think you're all set to fight? Now you'll want to find a gym. You can battle pokémon in both rival and allied gyms, but we'd recommend you take on a location that's controlled by a different team than your own to get a full-taste of what's to come. Plus, you get more XP for fighting the enemy, rather than training with your own team, which will help you level up faster.

To engage with a rival gym, walk up to one on your map. Click on the top of the gym and scope out your competition by determining its prestige, which goes up every time a pokémon stationed in the gym defeats another player's pokémon. When that prestige bar fills up, the gym can level up and more trainers will be able to add their pokémon in to defend it.

Now you can press the battle button. Your pokémon instantly finds itself in the battle arena, surrounded by the colors of the gym's controlling team. Your pokémon will be situated directly across from its opponent. On the top left corner of the screen is your pokémon's health meter, with your opponent's health displayed on the top right corner of the screen. Press on your opponent's pokémon over and over again on your phone as fast as you can to unleash your pokémon's quick attack on it. You can also dodge attacks by swiping left to right where your own pokémon is standing (or flying), so you might want to use two fingers when you battle. Different pokémon have different attack speeds and strength, so you may want to experiment with a wide variety of monsters to see which ones fare best in a battle.

You'll also notice there are blue bars located underneath your pokémon's health meter. These will fill up as the battle progresses. When they're full, press and hold your screen immediately to unleash your

pokémon's special attack, which will narrow the focus of your screen and unleash a powerful blow on your opponent. Some pokémon have faster special attacks than others, so once again, prepare to experiment with what works best for you.

If your pokémon's health bar runs out mid-battle, it will faint, and your next pokémon in the battle lineup will immediately appear on the screen to pick up where the out-of-commission one left off. You can also swap out pokémon mid-battle by pressing the switch button (the one with the two arrows) on the right corner of your screen. This allows you to save a struggling pokémon that is about to fall in battle to a stronger opponent.

EXPERT ADVICE

Right now, Pokémon Go is structured in a way that allows anyone to take control of gyms, even if their opponents technically have much stronger pokémon on deck. In general, using CP scores to assess battle effectiveness is overrated. Go for type-matching advantage instead, and remember your computer-run opponents don't have that boost.

The match-ups below and to the far left are all good examples of trainers using pokémon types and IV stats for maximum effectiveness.

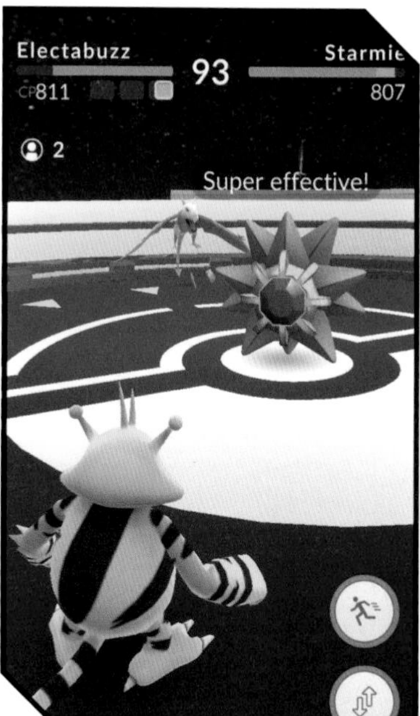

You'll gain XP for every pokémon you defeat in a battle, so even if you don't beat the entire gym, you'll still be rewarded for your efforts. Every time you beat all the pokémon in a gym, you'll reduce its prestige by around 2,000 points, potentially knocking it down one level and thereby knocking one pokémon out of the enemy lineup. A high-level gym with multiple pokémon

If there are no open gyms available to players on your team in your area, you may have to attempt to take an occupied one. Start off small and look for a low level gym first.

YOU WIN!

Wings and Ropes

Gym level 2

Gym Prestige

3936 / 4000

XP +350

Pokémon Defeated: 3

EXPERT ADVICE

Another way to win is through constant dodging. You can predict enemy attacks by watching for yellow flashes, which streak across the screen right before an opponent is about to land its attack. Swipe left or right whenever you see this visual cue. Also, because your enemies are using AI, they can't dodge your attacks, giving you the upper hand.

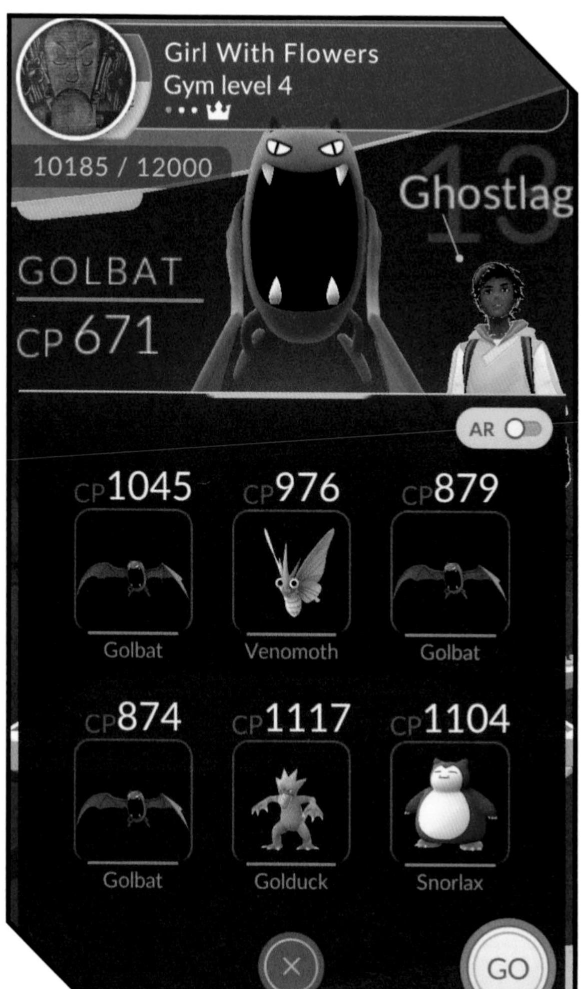

Each time you successfully defeat a rival gym's pokémon with one of your own, that gym loses around 2,000 prestige points. When it reaches zero, the gym is yours for the taking.

defenders requires multiple battles for you to take it over, giving rise to the kind of epic battle you post about on Reddit for bragging rights. That's why it's important to have a solid cache of potions in your backpack before you head into the gym. You can also heal all of your pokémon in between battles, so as long as you have six pokémon with relatively high CP—and plenty of healing tinctures—you'll have a fighting chance.

Teamwork can be a beautiful (and effective) tactic in tough gym battles, as seen with the two Jolteon taking on a Lapras (left) and a Jolteon/ Slowbro duo against a Vaporeon.

EXPERT ADVICE

Every level you advance in the game has a corresponding CP multiplier value. When you first catch a pokémon it will have a base multiplier value that corresponds to your level. As you level up, a pokémon's CP multiplier will continue to rise along with you, allowing you to build up more powerful pokémon as you advance in the game.

You can also team up with other players of your faction to take down a gym together. To do so, set your lineup and press the battle button on the lower right corner of your gym screen at the exact same time as another player (or players!). You'll see their pokémon across the battlefield also attacking your rival and you'll be able to double-, triple- or quadruple-team an opponent. Whenever you get the chance, roll through the gym with some battle buddies. Fighting as a pair at a Level 3 gym will pit 12

The most important part of a gym battle is setting a lineup that you think will match up against the roster of pokémon currently guarding the gym. Check the chart on page 154 for hints as to the best combos.

pokémon against three; with four trainers, that ratio hits a massive 24 against three. **Obviously, teamwork will significantly raise your chances of victory in a battle.**

Once a rival gym's prestige has hit zero, the gym will turn white on your screen and you will be able to take it over for your own faction. Act fast. Press on this empty gym immediately and hit the button on the lower left corner of the screen to put your pokémon in to defend it. You can only station pokémon with full health to defend your team's gym, so make sure you either have an undamaged pokémon on deck or revive/heal your pokémon with potions before you try to station it there.

For more information about how to defend a gym you're in control of once you've defeated the enemy, check out the next chapter, which goes into some of the more advanced strategies behind battling and gives tips on how to become the most poké-proficient trainer in your neighborhood.

ASSEMBLE YOUR DREAM TEAM

A trainer's most important decision is which pokémon to deploy in battle. Read on and never make the wrong choice again.

With the help of its Inner Focus, Dragonite can be one of the most powerful pokémon in a battle against almost any other creature, save against ice, rock and other dragon and fairy types. Attack this gym with caution.

The CP of your pokémon is just the tip of the iceberg when it comes to determining their worth in a gym battle. The game not only assigns distinct type advantages to every pokémon, but it also imbues the monsters with a number of "hidden stats" that master trainers and pokémon code-nerds have teased out of the game's internal data multiple times since Pokémon Go was first released. While these secret numbers are not necessarily essential for average players to win gym battles, for trainers who want to take things to the next level, it can add an extra skill set that might help give you an edge in some of your closer competitions.

EXPERT ADVICE

Every pokémon has a varying height and weight. Sometimes, these stats fall within the normal parameters for a species. However, some pokémon have a special XS or XL status. According to battle reports, these might have to do with attack speed and strength, with XS pokémon attacking faster, and XL pokémon hitting harder than normal in a battle.

Fire-type pokémon like Ponyta (left, foreground) and Growlithe (right, foreground) can be vulnerable to some water types but well suited to beating grass types, depending on level.

First things first: Every area has a slightly different array of pokémon that are common in the wild. For example, in places like New York City, there are a lot of grass, water and psychic type pokémon. In California, there are far more fire and ground types running around in the game. Ultimately, this means trainers who control gyms are far more likely to be battling with pokémon that are common to their area, especially starting out. Your aim as a master trainer should be to collect and build up the CP of pokémon that are "super effective" against these common types and to match them up accordingly in every gym battle you fight. So, even though they could be a rare find in the area, a trainer in the Big Apple may want to seek out and spend their extra stardust on building up some strong fire, ghost and dragon types. Meanwhile, those out west may want to focus on building a solid unit of water types for their battle roster.

When battling, especially against larger or higher-level pokémon, it's important to remember to dodge first, which allows you to get the essential first hit.

In a broader topographical sense, if you live near a lot of fields or parks where grass pokémon are common, you would be wise to stock up on poison, flying, bug or dragon pokémon. This type-matching strategy is why Golbats—one of the first pokémon you are likely to evolve due to the relative abundance of Zubats in the game—are incredibly good fighters against pokémon such as Bulbasaurs and Tangelas in a battle. The fanged monsters owe their battle advantage to their combined flying/poison status, which gives them the edge over grass-type herbivores.

Just because a pokémon is smaller than its opponent, like Sandshrew in the example below, it doesn't mean it's doomed in battle. Choose your fighters wisely and you might find that bigger pokémon are just as likely to lose.

However, if you live in an area surrounded by parking lots or industrial buildings, that same defeated Bulbasaur can come in handy, as the attacks of grass-type pokémon are super effective against the ground types that likely frequent your neighborhood. **In this way, the Pokémon Go game seems to favor exploratory trainers who track down pokémon in a variety of different biomes and locales.**

EXPERT ADVICE

The highest level a gym can currently achieve in the game is Level 10, which means there can be a maximum of 10 pokémon defenders at any location. Unless you have a team of six high CP pokémon fighters, defeating these power-houses will most likely take some teamwork, plus plenty of potions to heal your pokémon between rounds.

Another easy way to strategize by pokémon type? Determine what type of pokémon dominate the gyms in your area. Once you have, build up your battle lineup to reflect the exact opposite. For example, if you want to knock your neighbor's super-strong Snorlax out of a rival gym, you're going to want to plan an attack with a fighting-type pokémon such as Hitmonchan, who can take down normal-type pokémon a lot easier than it does others.

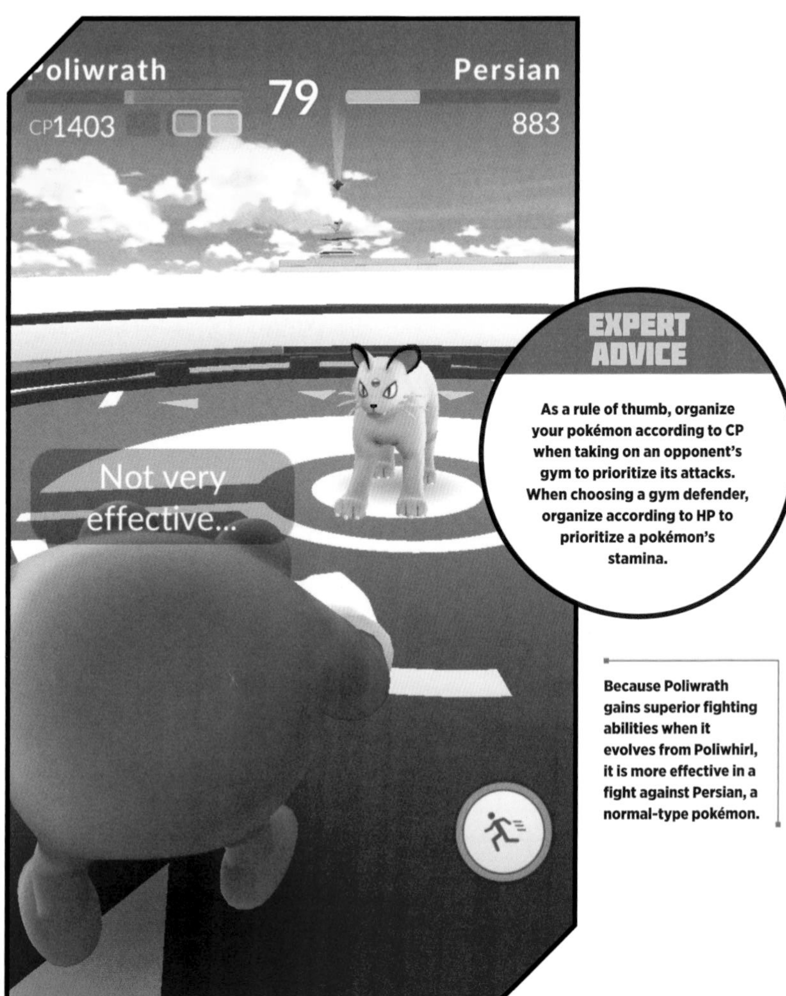

EXPERT ADVICE

As a rule of thumb, organize your pokémon according to CP when taking on an opponent's gym to prioritize its attacks. When choosing a gym defender, organize according to HP to prioritize a pokémon's stamina.

Because Poliwrath gains superior fighting abilities when it evolves from Poliwhirl, it is more effective in a fight against Persian, a normal-type pokémon.

Golduck's type advantage gives Flareon a tough battle in the above example. Similarly, Starmie's powers are able to overwhelm the fiery puppy pokémon Arcanine.

Charmander can demolish a grass type like Bulbasaur, but Squirtle can school the former if matched in an equal CP battle. The whole affair resembles a game of rock-paper-scissors, where certain pokémon (even if they technically have a lower CP) can absolutely destroy another type they are strong against. For a quick reference on what types of pokémon battle best against others, consult the chart on page 154.

EXPERT ADVICE

Try to attack higher-level gyms late at night or during other off-hours, when rival defenders are less likely to be stationed nearby to build back up the location's prestige. Try to learn the habits of other top trainers in your area. For the most part, controlling gyms is easier during the week, when people are at work or in school.

Got your ultimate battle roster set for your area? Further down the line, once you've collected dozens of different types and evolutions of pokémon, it may be a good idea to build up the battle CP of one of each type of pokémon. That way, you can strategically match up your roster of fighters for every battle, not just on a larger location-based scale. Remember: at enemy

A Golbat might not be at the top of your wish list, but if you train it right and pay close attention to building its CP, it could be your hidden ace in the hole against certain types.

gyms, you have six pokémon to battle with, and you can swap this roster out in a fight at any time. So, if you see a gym full of Vaporeons, counter with an army of Volteons, Raichus and Golems. But if a rival trainer throws in a Charizard to help defend their position later on, swap out your electric types for a Blastoise or a Poliwrath and witness its destruction.

Sometimes, rival gyms pack a wide variety of pokémon types, which is good strategy because it ensures no one subset of pokémon can bring it down. That's why it's important for every master trainer to fill their battle roster with a variety of different monsters. You want to be prepared for any combination of battle at any moment. So even if you think fairy pokémon like Clefable and Wigglytuff might damage your image as a hardcore master trainer, you may want to keep a few on deck in case

Given that several pokémon are dual-type pokémon, and that many of the monsters can perform moves of multiple types, picking the right pokémon is anything but simple. Fairy-type Jigglypuff may possess moves effective against fighting-type Machoke, but the latter's fighting-type attacks and higher CP score carries the day.

you come upon a wicked fighting type like Primape or the deadly Hitmonlee in the midst of a battle. If you play long enough, you'll start to memorize these type advantages and also notice which of your pokémon seem to be unbeatable in a battle.

EXPERT ADVICE

You can only station one defending pokémon per gym, but you can use however many pokémon you want to defend multiple gyms at once. This will require some walking and a couple of allied trainers. Work together to level up a gym as high as possible before moving on to the next location if you want to run the neighborhood.

That brings us to another important consideration of building your ultimate battle dream team: the game's "hidden stats." Ever since the original Game Boy cartridges came out in the mid-'90s, pokémon enthusiasts have been picking apart the game's internal code and running long-term statistical studies to determine which monsters are the best battlers, down to even the most minute percentages. But the interesting thing about Pokémon Go is that it turns a lot of the original game's secret stats on their heads, fueling a massive push by pokémon data nerds to unlock the new rules of battle.

Gamers at websites such as The Silph Road and on Reddit have already gone into the game's internal code files, publishing their findings of a wide array

Even though official rankings have shed some light on which pokémon does better against another, you never know who's going to win until the fight is underway.

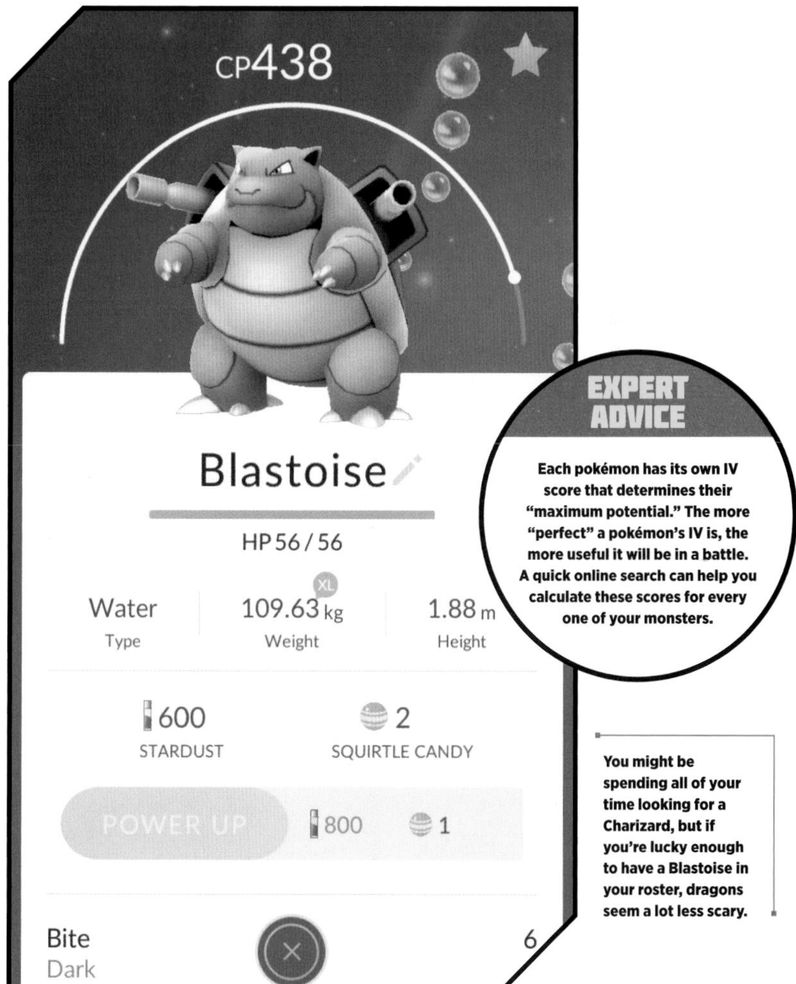

EXPERT ADVICE

Each pokémon has its own IV score that determines their "maximum potential." The more "perfect" a pokémon's IV is, the more useful it will be in a battle. A quick online search can help you calculate these scores for every one of your monsters.

You might be spending all of your time looking for a Charizard, but if you're lucky enough to have a Blastoise in your roster, dragons seem a lot less scary.

of secret stats from a massive "data dump" published less than a week after the game was first released in the United States. The stats were later updated after the game shifted its battle stats in a major update a few weeks after Pokémon Go's release. These programming-savvy trainers continue to release updated rankings of the "strongest" pokémon in the mobile version of the game, determined by weighing a dizzying array of battle statistics not listed in the game's main play screens, as well as lists of every possible attack a pokémon can have.

Here's the gist of how these lineups have been determined: Every pokémon has invisible stats behind its battle capabilities, called individual values or IVs. Veteran pokémon players will recognize that IVs have been around since the original games and include factors such as base attack, base defense and pokémon stamina or "energy". These numbers are independent of the pokémon's main CP, so in a battle, even pokémon at the same combat level could fight very differently, giving one a distinct hidden advantage. If down the line, you end up battling your Charizard with a Dragonite of the same exact CP value, expect the former dragon to have a more difficult fight.

Though Snorlax's thick fat gives it an incredible immunity to injury from any physical attack, against a pokémon with psychic attacks like Golduck these qualities are less valuable.

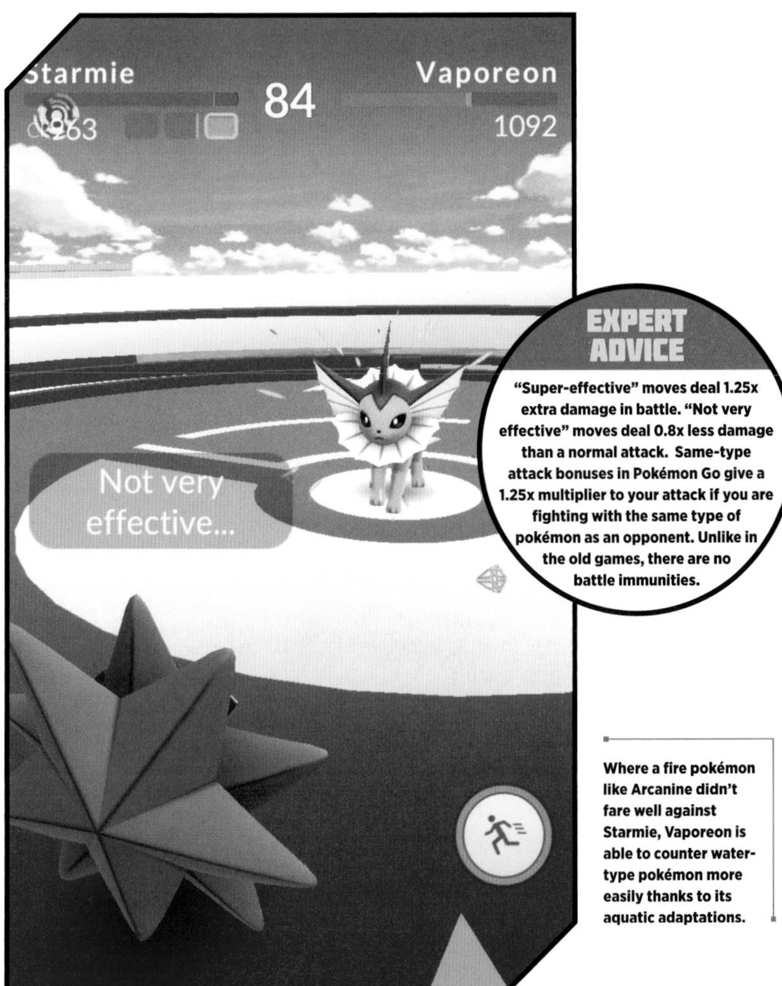

EXPERT ADVICE

"Super-effective" moves deal 1.25x extra damage in battle. "Not very effective" moves deal 0.8x less damage than a normal attack. Same-type attack bonuses in Pokémon Go give a 1.25x multiplier to your attack if you are fighting with the same type of pokémon as an opponent. Unlike in the old games, there are no battle immunities.

Where a fire pokémon like Arcanine didn't fare well against Starmie, Vaporeon is able to counter water-type pokémon more easily thanks to its aquatic adaptations.

On the other hand, if an epic battle between a CP-balanced Mew and Mewtwo ever occurs in the history of Pokémon Go, expect the battle outcome to turn out way worse for Mew than it did in the original *Pokémon* movie. These adjusted (and re-adjusted) IV lineups have enraged a lot of long-time pokémon players, who argue that these new hidden stats continue to throw off the crucial balance of the game they know and love.

EXPERT ADVICE

Every move in Pokémon Go also has a special damage-per-second, or DPS, stat. In general, moves with higher power will have slower attack speeds. Find a balance between speed and power. If you're looking for pokémon with especially high DPS, consider Golem, Wigglytuff, Parasect, Dragonite or Starmie.

One of the only times in the game of Pokémon Go that a toss up occurs is when two pokémon of the same species battle each other. But even then, high CP or IV levels mean some are better.

But you're here to play Pokémon Go and win, not argue with programmer pokétrainers about the pros and cons of its game design. Know this: No matter how much you power up your favorite pokémon, its IV scores will remain the same. So even if you have one 400 CP Charizard and one 30 CP Charizard, their hidden battle stats may actually reveal that the latter will be a more formidable battler with a bit of work put into it.

Delving even more deeply into it, a pokémon's base attack helps determine how much damage it can dole out per battle. Conversely, a pokémon's base defense determines how much damage a pokémon takes when it is hit with an attack. Stamina, the most intriguing stat of all, is what's represented by HP as well as the blue bar located under your pokémon's HP bar that slowly fills up during a battle and eventually doles out its special attack. Higher stamina means a pokémon will last longer in battle and that its stronger special attack will refuel more quickly throughout the fight, awarding it a higher DPS, or "damage per second" score. That's huge in Pokémon Go, as one special attack can have the ability to completely wipe an opponent battleground in one hit, and you'll definitely want your pokémon to hit first.

Although Clefable (center) has a higher species defense than the attacking Vaporeon, the latter's superior DPS means it can unleash a devastating special attack much quicker.

From the Silph Road's super-detailed findings we can determine some common themes in the Pokémon Go battle arena: Fire-type pokémon in general dominate the top 10 attackers in the game, making up four of the highest DPS monsters in the game. Plant-type pokémon come in second, contributing two pokémon, Exeggutor

From left: Many pokémon with great species stats happen to be water-type pokémon, but that's why you should bring grass and electric types with you to any battle; electric types Jolteon and Magneton can help put the hurt on strong water-type pokémon, such as this Vaporeon.

and Victreebel, to the top 10 DPS list. Water pokémon, which dominated the game prior to its massive update at the end of July, still hold their own in the top 20 but have been dramatically "nerfed" or had their attack powers weakened to help even the playing field in the battle arena. Electric-, rock-, fairy- and bug-type pokémon appear relatively infrequently in the top attackers list, so maybe pass on powering up your Pinsir.

EXPERT ADVICE

Cross-chop, a fighting-type attack, has recently overtaken Water Gun as the highest DPS move in the game. Other notable strong attacks include Stone Edge, Body Slam, Blizzard, Power Whip and Megahorn, so keep an eye out for pokémon who pack them.

To find a full list of these stats for each and every pokémon in the game, check out our Strengh in Numbers chart on page 156. However, don't get too worried about crunching the numbers for each of your pokémon. With a little bit of teamwork and some creative type-matching, you're still relatively likely to win a battle, even if your pokémon have lower IV, DPS or CP scores. And that's where the battle dynamics of Pokémon Go get really interesting.

Think about the way Pokémon Go gym battles are currently set up: A Level 5 gym (a relatively strong bastion of defense) can contain a maximum of five pokémon to defend it. However, each rival challenger can use six of their own pokémon to attack it. What's more, multiple players can team up to defeat a gym's pokémon together. So even if a

This Nidoking may be able to take out this Magikarp with ease, but know that other low-level pokémon can defeat anyone in large enough numbers. Nidoking will be in bigger trouble if the attacker deploys a ground-type pokémon, which he is weak against.

team has five 1000+ CP pokémon with some of the highest IV scores defending it, a team of four amatuer rival trainers who have pokémon with half the CP power could still technically take the gym down if they pool their pokémon together and overwhelm the gym with sheer determination and numbers. No matter how good your defending pokémon are, a fight that pits 20 pokémon against five doesn't look good for the home team.

EXPERT ADVICE

Building a Level 10 gym takes a lot of time, but breaking it down takes a fraction of that work. Know that the CPU only pushes to attack once every 1.5 seconds, which is generally much slower than the attack rate of most real life pokémon trainers, so you not only have a numbers advantage, you have a timing advantage, too.

EXPERT ADVICE

Nidoking is great and all, but Snorlax may be one of your best bets as a gym defender. It has relatively high HP compared to other pokémon, meaning it will last longer in a battle. Snorlax also attacks fairly quickly, especially for its size. If you're lucky enough to get one with a strong Body Slam attack, even better. I've seen this move halve a rival's HP in one blow.

This trainer is clearly in Team Mystic territory, meaning any rival teams on the prowl will have to stick together to defend any gyms they take over.

This is why it's relatively easy to take over a gym in Pokémon Go (especially if you have a lot of friends), but a lot harder to defend it for any significant amount of time. If you do plan on holding a gym for more than about five seconds when your neighborhood is swarming with rivals, you're going to have to stay put with your team and train in it.

Training at an allied gym helps build up your own XP and boost a gym's prestige, which eventually allows you to level up the gym and add in more pokémon to defend it. As soon as you take control of a gym, have everyone on your team start training. When you train at an allied location, you only get to use one pokémon to battle the entire gym lineup, so make sure you still have at least one strong pokémon in your fighting roster that is not assigned to a gym. You will not earn any prestige or XP if your training pokémon can't even get past your team's first defender, so maybe don't put your absolute best pokémon in a gym to defend it if you know you're planning on training for a bit. In fact, some trainer teams will purposely put one weak, or low CP pokémon, in the gym as "sacrifice" to ensure that every training session they attempt is successful. That way, they can level up their gym faster and add in more pokémon to defend it ASAP. So don't laugh if you see a CP 50 Rattata as the first battler at your local gym. It could be followed by an epic team of much higher CP pokémon put there by a team of master strategists.

This relatively weak Sandshrew makes a perfect sparring partner for allied team members trying to level up a gym. The team just better have stronger pokémon in reserve.

Also, if you see an allied gym that will allow you to put one of your own pokémon in to defend it, pick a pokémon that is of a different type than any of the other monsters you see currently stationed there. Remember: A gym boasting a variety of pokémon types is a harder gym to take down. The more you train and win at an allied gym, the harder it will be for other teams to take it back, so be prepared to work the gym beat for a long time if you really want to be a master battler.

EXPERT ADVICE

The best way to maximize your gym bonus for free pokécoins is to take a bunch of gyms in a very short amount of time during non-peak hours, and then start collecting right away. For instance, going gym-to-gym at 6 in the morning (on a bike) once yielded me control of four gyms at once. By the end of the day, all my pokémon were knocked out.

Don't underestimate the battle prowess of fairy-type pokémon such as this Jigglypuff. They are important for keeping the gym defenders well-rounded (pun intended).

When all else fails, sometimes the best tactic is to mob a gym with friends. This poor Clefable doesn't stand a chance against the tag-team of Sandslash and Magmar.

At the end of the day, the best way to win a gym battle is by combining this multitude of tactics together. Start by matching your pokémon by type for every battle and every location you're battling in. Familiarize yourself with each pokémon's secret IV stats (or at least the theories behind them) to maximize your success. Then, link up with some buddies and take on rival gyms together. A solid crew of trainers cooperating is the real unstoppable force in Pokémon Go.

PLAYING TO TYPE

We detail every pokémon type's basic/essential strengths and weaknesses to give you the edge you need in any gym battle.

In Pokémon Go, just as in previous incarnations of the game, certain types do better than others against each type. It can sometimes be like trying to compete in the most complex game of rock-paper-scissors of all time, but with this handy chart, we've laid down a basic strategy for you.

POKÉMON TYPE	GOOD AGAINST	WEAK AGAINST
BUG	Grass, Psychic	Fire, Flying, Rock, Ghost, Steel, Fairy
DRAGON	Fire, Water, Electric, Grass	Ice, Dragon, Fairy, Steel
ELECTRIC	Water, Flying	Ground, Steel, Grass, Dragon
FAIRY	Fighting, Dragon	Poison, Steel, Fire
FIGHTING	Normal, Ice, Rock, Steel	Fairy, Psychic, Flying, Poison
FIRE	Grass, Ice, Bug, Steel	Water, Ground, Rock, Dragon
FLYING	Grass, Fighting, Bug	Electric, Ice, Rock, Steel
GHOST	Psychic, Ghost	No disadvantages
GRASS	Water, Ground, Rock	Fire, Ice, Poison, Flying, Bug, Dragon
GROUND	Fire, Electric, Poison, Rock, Steel	Water, Ice, Grass, Bug
ICE	Grass, Ground, Flying, Dragon	Fire, Water, Rock, Fighting, Steel
NORMAL	No advantages	Fighting, Rock, Steel, Ghost
POISON	Grass, Fairy	Ground, Psychic, Steel, Rock
PSYCHIC	Fighting, Poison	Psychic, Bug, Ghost
ROCK	Fire, Ice, Flying, Bug	Fighting, Ground, Steel, Water
STEEL	Ice, Rock, Fairy	Fire, Water, Fighting, Ground
WATER	Fire, Ground, Rock	Electric, Grass, Dragon

EXPERT ADVICE

Some pokémon have attacks that are different than their type. For example, some poison/ground-type Nidokings might be packing a special Megahorn attack, which is technically a bug-type move. In these instances, the attack type matters more than the pokémon type for gaining an attack advantage in a gym battle. However, its defense will not be affected.

By carefully analyzing your pokémon and keeping dual types especially in mind, it's possible to give yourself a distinct advantage over someone who picks their pokémon based solely on past experience. Of course, CP and other factors enter into the equation, but type is a huge factor.

STRENGTH IN NUMBERS

EXPERT ADVICE

When defending gyms, a pokémon with a lower CP but a higher defense and stamina stat may be a better pick than a higher CP pokémon that just has a really high attack. For attacking, don't worry about picking a pokémon with a low defense score. You can always dodge to avoid taking a hit.

Research from grassroots network The Silph Road ranks every pokémon by their best combined statistics.

POKÉMON	BEST FAST MOVE	BEST SPECIAL MOVE	ATTACK	DEFENSE	STAMINA
MEWTWO	Psycho Cut	Psychic	284	202	212
DRAGONITE	Dragon Breath	Dragon Claw	250	212	182
EXEGGUTOR	Zen Headbutt	Solar Beam	232	164	190
ARCANINE	Fire Fang	Fire Blast	230	180	180
MOLTRES	Ember	Fire Blast	242	194	180
CHARIZARD	Wing Attack	Fire Blast	212	182	156
FLAREON	Ember	Fire Blast	238	178	130
ZAPDOS	Thunder Shock	Thunder	232	194	180
VICTREEBEL	Razor Leaf	Solar Beam	222	152	160
MEW	Pound	Psychic	220	220	200
STARMIE	Water Gun	Hydro Pump	194	192	120
GOLDUCK	Water Gun	Hydro Pump	194	176	160
VENUSAUR	Vine Whip	Solar Beam	198	200	160
NIDOKING	Poison Jab	Earthquake	204	170	162
BLASTOISE	Water Gun	Hydro Pump	186	222	158
VAPOREON	Water Gun	Hydro Pump	186	168	260

KEY

NORMAL
WATER
ELECTRIC
FIRE
GRASS
FLYING
PSYCHIC
ICE
DRAGON
POISON
FIGHTING
GROUND
ROCK
FAIRY
BUG
STEEL
GHOST

POKÉMON	BEST FAST MOVE	BEST SPECIAL MOVE	ATTACK	DEFENSE	STAMINA
GOLEM	Mud Shot	Stone Edge	176	198	160
ARTICUNO	Frost Breath	Blizzard	198	242	180
VILEPLUME	Razor Leaf	Solar Beam	202	190	150
MAGMAR	Ember	Fire Blast	214	158	130
WIGGLYTUFF	Pound	Hyper Beam	168	108	280
OMASTAR	Water Gun	Hydro Pump	180	202	140
CLOYSTER	Frost Breath	Blizzard	196	196	100
KABUTOPS	Mud Shot	Stone Edge	190	190	120
RAICHU	Spark	Thunder	200	154	120
ALAKAZAM	Psycho Cut	Psychic	186	152	110
SLOWBRO	Water Gun	Psychic	184	198	190
SEADRA	Water Gun	Hydro Pump	176	150	110
GYARADOS	Dragon Breath	Hydro Pump	192	196	190
NIDOQUEEN	Poison Jab	Earthquake	184	190	180
PARASECT	Bug Bite	Solar Beam	162	170	120
LAPRAS	Frost Breath	Blizzard	186	190	260
ELECTABUZZ	Thunder Shock	Thunder	198	160	130
RAPIDASH	Ember	Fire Blast	200	170	130
GENGAR	Shadow Claw	Sludge Wave	204	156	120
JOLTEON	Thunder Shock	Thunder	192	174	130
MUK	Poison Jab	Sludge Bomb	180	188	210
POLIWRATH	Bubble	Hydro Pump	180	202	180
WEEPINBELL	Razor Leaf	Sludge Bomb	190	110	130
RHYDON	Mud Slap	Stone Edge	166	160	210
DRAGONAIR	Dragon Breath	Dragon Pulse	170	152	122
VENOMOTH	Bug Bite	Bug Buzz	172	154	140
TANGELA	Vine Whip	Solar Beam	164	152	130
PIDGEOT	Wing Attack	Hurricane	170	166	166
SNORLAX	Lick	Hyper Beam	180	180	320
TENTACRUEL	Poison Jab	Hydro Pump	170	196	160
CLEFABLE	Pound	Moonblast	178	178	190
AERODACTYL	Bite	Hyper Beam	182	162	160
HAUNTER	Lick	Sludge Bomb	172	118	90
MAGNETON	Spark	Flash Cannon	186	180	100
IVYSAUR	Vine Whip	Solar Beam	156	158	120
WEEZING	Tackle	Sludge Bomb	190	198	130
NINETALES	Ember	Fire Blast	176	194	146
GRAVELER	Mud Shot	Stone Edge	142	156	110
MACHAMP	Karate Chop	Cross Chop	198	180	180
WARTORTLE	Water Gun	Hydro Pump	144	176	118
SANDSLASH	Mud Shot	Earthquake	150	172	150
DEWGONG	Frost Breath	Blizzard	156	192	180
BELLSPROUT	Vine Whip	Sludge Bomb	158	78	100
PONYTA	Ember	Fire Blast	168	138	100
DUGTRIO	Mud Shot	Earthquake	148	140	70

POKÉMON	BEST FAST MOVE	BEST SPECIAL MOVE	ATTACK	DEFENSE	STAMINA
HYPNO	Zen Headbutt	Psychic	162	196	170
RATICATE	Bite	Hyper Beam	146	150	110
BEEDRILL	Bug Bite	Sludge Bomb	144	130	130
SCYTHER	Steel Wing	Bug Buzz	176	180	140
GLOOM	Razor Leaf	Petal Blizzard	162	158	120
CHARMELEON	Scratch	Flamethrower	160	140	116
PRIMEAPE	Low Kick	Cross Chop	178	150	130
PINSIR	Fury Cutter	X-Scissor	184	186	130
ARBOK	Bite	Gunk Shot	166	166	120
JYNX	Pound	Psyshock	172	134	130
MR. MIME	Zen Headbutt	Psychic	154	196	80
GROWLITHE	Bite	Flamethrower	156	110	110
BUTTERFREE	Bug Bite	Bug Buzz	144	144	120
DODRIO	Feint Attack	Drill Peck	182	150	120
NIDORINO	Poison Sting	Sludge Bomb	142	128	122
ELECTRODE	Spark	Thunderbolt	150	174	120
PERSIAN	Scratch	Play Rough	156	146	130
KINGLER	Metal Claw	X-Scissor	178	168	110
MAROWAK	Mud Slap	Earthquake	140	202	120
HITMONLEE	Rock Smash	Stone Edge	148	172	100
SEAKING	Poison Jab	Megahorn	172	160	160
PSYDUCK	Water Gun	Cross Chop	132	112	100
NIDORINA	Poison Sting	Sludge Bomb	132	136	140
GASTLY	Lick	Sludge Bomb	136	82	60
GOLBAT	Wing Attack	Poison Fang	164	164	150
TAUROS	Tackle	Earthquake	148	184	150
MACHOKE	Low Kick	Cross Chop	154	144	160
HITMONCHAN	Rock Smash	Brick Break	138	204	100
FEAROW	Steel Wing	Drill Run	168	146	130
BULBASAUR	Vine Whip	Sludge Bomb	126	126	90
ODDISH	Razor Leaf	Sludge Bomb	134	130	90
KADABRA	Psycho Cut	Shadow Ball	150	112	80
MANKEY	Scratch	Cross Chop	122	96	80
MAGNEMITE	Spark	Thunderbolt	128	138	50
CHARMANDER	Scratch	Flamethrower	128	108	78
LICKITUNG	Lick	Hyper Beam	126	160	180
FARFETCH'D	Cut	Leaf Blade	138	132	104
PORYGON	Tackle	Signal Beam	156	158	130
KOFFING	Tackle	Sludge Bomb	136	142	80
PARAS	Bug Bite	Seed Bomb	122	120	70
PIKACHU	Thunder Shock	Thunder	124	108	70
DRATINI	Dragon Breath	Aqua Tail	128	110	82
SLOWPOKE	Water Gun	Psychic	110	110	180
MEOWTH	Scratch	Body Slam	104	94	80
EKANS	Poison Sting	Sludge Bomb	112	112	70

POKÉMON	BEST FAST MOVE	BEST SPECIAL MOVE	ATTACK	DEFENSE	STAMINA
POLIWHIRL	Bubble	Scald	132	132	130
KANGASKHAN	Mud Slap	Earthquake	142	178	210
NIDORAN(M)	Poison Sting	Sludge Bomb	110	94	92
JIGGLYPUFF	Pound	Body Slam	98	54	230
CLEFAIRY	Pound	Moonblast	116	124	140
HORSEA	Water Gun	Dragon Pulse	122	100	60
EEVEE	Tackle	Body Slam	114	128	110
GRIMER	Mud Slap	Sludge Bomb	124	110	160
SEEL	Water Gun	Aqua Tail	104	138	130
SQUIRTLE	Bubble	Aqua Tail	112	142	88
KABUTO	Scratch	Aqua Jet	148	142	60
NIDORAN(F)	Poison Sting	Sludge Bomb	100	104	110
STARYU	Water Gun	Power Gem	130	128	60
DROWZEE	Pound	Psychic	104	140	120
MACHOP	Low Kick	Cross Chop	118	96	140
EXEGGCUTE	Confusion	Psychic	110	132	120
OMANYTE	Water Gun	Brine	132	160	70
POLIWAG	Bubble	Body Slam	108	98	80
VOLTORB	Spark	Thunderbolt	102	124	80
VENONAT	Bug Bite	Signal Beam	108	118	120
GOLDEEN	Mud Shot	Aqua Tail	112	126	90
DODUO	Peck	Drill Peck	126	96	70
ABRA	Zen Headbutt	Psyshock	110	76	50
PIDGEOTTO	Wing Attack	Aerial Ace	126	122	126
VULPIX	Ember	Flamethrower	106	118	76
ONIX	Rock Throw	Stone Edge	90	186	70
GEODUDE	Rock Throw	Rock Slide	106	118	80
RATTATA	Tackle	Body Slam	92	86	60
CUBONE	Mud Slap	Bone Club	102	150	100
ZUBAT	Bite	Sludge Bomb	88	90	80
DIGLETT	Mud Shot	Dig	108	86	20
KRABBY	Bubble	Water Pulse	116	110	60
RHYHORN	Mud Slap	Stomp	110	116	160
DITTO	Pound	Struggle	110	110	96
SHELLDER	Tackle	Water Pulse	120	112	60
SPEAROW	Peck	Drill Peck	102	78	80
TENTACOOL	Bubble	Water Pulse	106	136	80
SANDSHREW	Mud Shot	Rock Slide	90	114	100
PIDGEY	Tackle	Aerial Ace	94	90	80
WEEDLE	Bug Bite	Struggle	68	64	80
KAKUNA	Poison Jab	Struggle	62	82	90
CHANSEY	Pound	Psychic	40	60	500
CATERPIE	Bug Bite	Struggle	62	66	90
METAPOD	Bug Bite	Struggle	56	86	100
MAGIKARP	Splash	Struggle	42	84	40

Source: ***thesilphroad.com***

TEAM PLAYER

Joining a faction opens up a whole new world within Pokémon Go.

Pokémon Go lets you live out your fantasy of becoming a legendary pokémon trainer, but even more thrilling is how the app encourages you to share that dream with millions of others. Besides the countless stories of Pokémon Go bringing together trainers who would otherwise remain total strangers (see page 190 for the most touching of these tales), the app prompts trainers to join up with one of three factions to instill some team pride. In a short span of time, these teams have already taken on identities of their own to make its members feel like they are invested in a living, growing community of trainers.

You're prompted to choose your team as soon as your trainer reaches Level 5. Here's the rundown on Pokémon Go's factions, including their fictional, in-game leaders, pokémon mascots and driving philosophies toward catching them all.

When a trainer reaches Level 7, they receive 15 pokéballs, 10 potions, five revives and an incense.

EXPERT ADVICE

Phones that are jail-broken will allow players to switch to other apps on their smartphones while playing without closing out the game. That being said, this hack will void your phone's warranty, so do so at your own risk.

TEAM INSTINCT

Led by Sparks, Team Instinct is all about—you guessed it—following your gut. He also believes pokémon have fantastic intuition and this is how they know when to hatch out of eggs. If you think you're going to rely on your spidey-senses in battle, join this team. Instinct's mascot is the legendary bird pokémon Zapdos, known for its ability to stir up storms and gain power if it's struck by lightning.

TEAM MYSTIC

If you're intrigued by the idea behind pokémon's evolution, the blue Team Mystic might be right for you. Blanche, who leads the team, is the definition of cool, calm and collected. Instead of charging into battle, she approaches it logically and weighs her situation carefully. Speaking of cool, Mystic's mascot is ice-cold. It's Articuno, the legendary bird pokémon who makes it snow just by flying through the air.

So far, Team Mystic is the most popular squad in Pokémon Go. This means finding allied gyms is easy, but finding places to battle can be difficult.

Part of the ethos of Team Valor is the belief that pokémon are stronger than the humans who train them and should be respected as such.

EXPERT ADVICE

The best way to use an incense to its fullest potential is to place it down at an already-activated lure site. That way, you'll get double the amount of pokémon coming your way, without ever having to move. If you're also hatching eggs, you can always walk around the lure sites in circles to try clocking more kilometers.

TEAM VALOR

If red is your power color, you might want to consider joining Team Valor. Led by Candela, Valor prizes power and strength in pokémon over everything else. Candela's goal is to figure out how to increase pokémon's natural powers. She wants to have the strongest pokémon defending her gym and ally with like-minded, fiercely competitive trainers. This team's mascot is the legendary bird Moltres, who can harness and control fire.

WHICH TO PICK?

The first thing to keep in mind is that none of the teams are different from each other as far as gameplay is concerned. However, that doesn't mean you should just blindly choose one of the three. If the descriptions of the teams don't sway you in a specific direction, choose a team based on the factors below. For example, if you live in an area where gyms are all dominated by

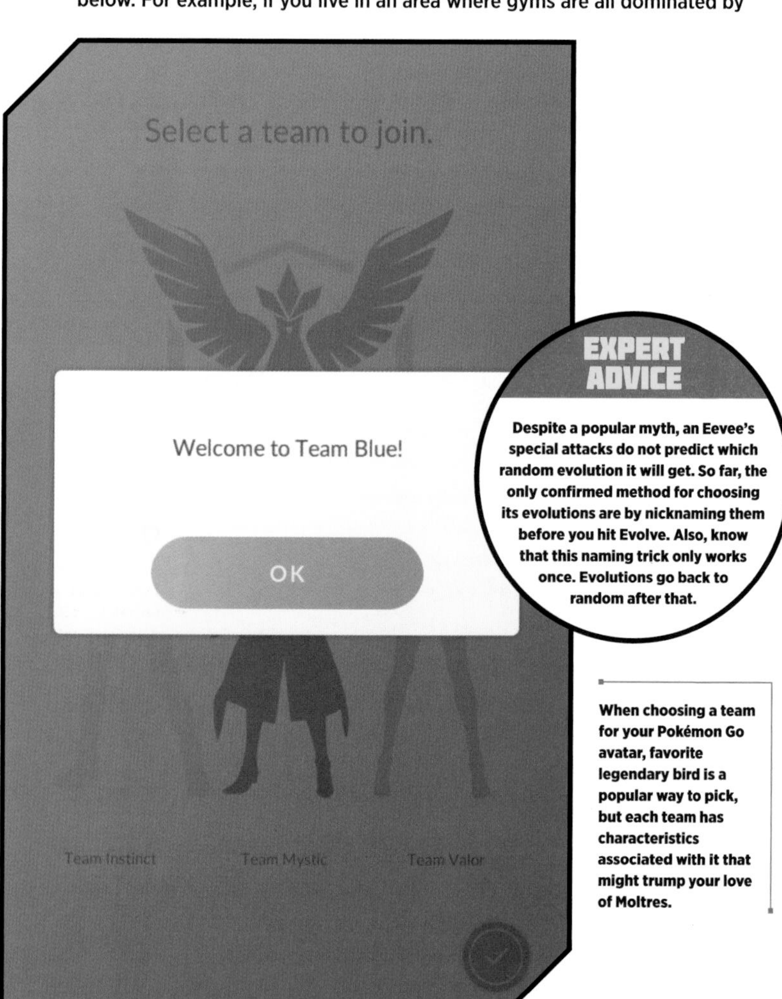

EXPERT ADVICE

Despite a popular myth, an Eevee's special attacks do not predict which random evolution it will get. So far, the only confirmed method for choosing its evolutions are by nicknaming them before you hit Evolve. Also, know that this naming trick only works once. Evolutions go back to random after that.

When choosing a team for your Pokémon Go avatar, favorite legendary bird is a popular way to pick, but each team has characteristics associated with it that might trump your love of Moltres.

Make sure to hit up pokéstops for potions to heal any of your pokémon that were injured in battle.

one team, it might make more sense to go with that team. However, if you like to be constantly fighting against enemies, you might want to join a team that doesn't control a gym in your area.

Now, let's say all three teams are represented in gyms in your area. If you still aren't sure which one to choose, take a look at some facts. Out of the three teams, Team Instinct currently has the least amount of players, while Team Mystic overwhelmingly has the most. Team Mystic also supposedly has the most dedicated players, so if you want to dive deep into Pokémon Go, there might be a chance that you'll also make new friends.

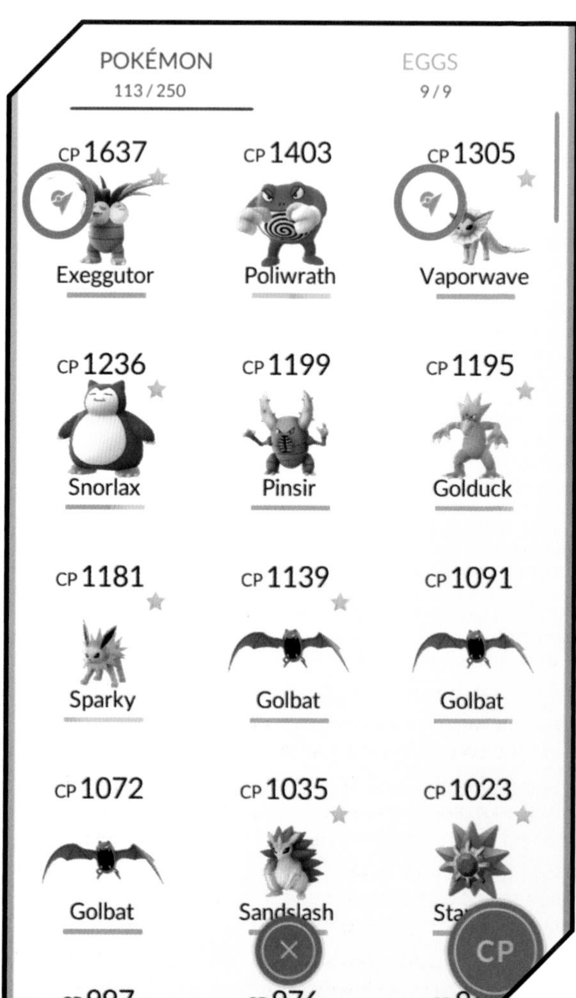

Once your pokédex starts getting full, you may be called upon to use a particularly prized monster to help guard a gym. The blue icon signifies that pokémon is defending a gym.

BEING A GOOD TEAMMATE

To be an asset to your team, you have to commit some time (and pokémon) to them. **If you want your team to keep control of its gym, it will need to have powerful pokémon defending it.** Leave one of your good pokémon at a friendly gym to help defend it, but don't necessarily leave your best. You won't be able to use the pokémon you left at your gym when you're battling at rival gyms.

Fire-type pokémon such as Magmar are resistant to a variety of attack types, making them useful in defending an allied gym.

EXPERT ADVICE

Hunting for pokémon in a pack also brings a searching advantage. Pokémon will sometimes show up on friends' screens before they do on yours, and they can point you in the right direction so you can capture them as well. On that note, it's always in good form to announce every pokémon you see to help out fellow trainers.

Next, be on the lookout if one of your teammates is attacking a rival gym and be sure to lend a hand. Sometimes, teams will coordinate attacks on social media pages they've created for the game in your area. To take over a gym, you and your team need to knock the gym's prestige down to zero. You can do this by battling six of your monsters against the rival gym's pokémon defenders. Defeating a gym is difficult as a solo premise but a cinch with some friends, so help out when you can (see page 120 for more tips on gym battles).

You shouldn't only check your team's social media accounts for battles. If you see a rare pokémon around, be a team player and use whatever channels you can to notify your teammates. If you share the wealth, your team will only get stronger. It doesn't help anyone if you keep all the fantastic pokémon to yourself.

By having a communicative team, you'll be prepared for an event that some Pokémon Go trainers believe will happen in the future. Some think the teams' association with the three legendary bird pokémon is no coincidence and that the team you choose will limit your ability to catch one of the three legendary birds. For example, Team Instinct users will only see and have the opportunity to capture Zapdos. Some users are predicting, based off of Niantic's first augmented reality game, "Ingress," that the legendary birds will appear and each respective team will have to work together to bring them in. For now, that remains one of the game's biggest mysteries.

GAMING THE SYSTEM

Want to get ahead in Pokémon Go and aren't concerned with ethics or fair play? These shortcuts and loopholes will get you there.

Pokémon Go has become a worldwide obsession for millions of fans around the world, transforming ordinary men, women and children into aspiring pokémon trainers in the blink of an eye. Most of them feel content capturing the Krabbys wandering through their office, evolving a few Pidgeys and checking out the nearby coffee shop to pick up some pokéballs. Maybe they once felt daring and challenged a Level 2 gym, with the predictable result of their Rattata/Zubat lineup getting wiped out.

But you, the trainer with enough foresight to purchase this field guide, are not a weekend poké-warrior. You're in this to become the best you can be, and that means taking advantage of every tip, trick and loophole in Pokémon Go's code. You're not a cheater—the lamest of the lame—but why should your diligent study of the ins and outs of the game go unrewarded? Even if you didn't necessarily put in the hours of experimentation to come up with the following creative solves to a trainer's most common problems, you can still avail yourself of these life hacks to

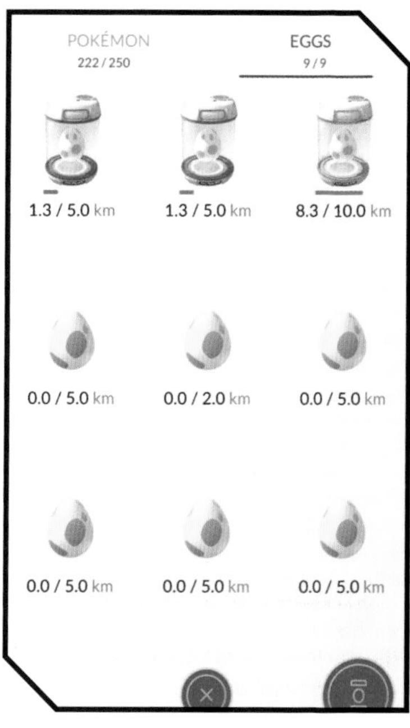

Extra inclubators can be a good investment if you happen to come across a surplus of eggs, but the one that you get at the beginning of the game should serve you well in less abundant times.

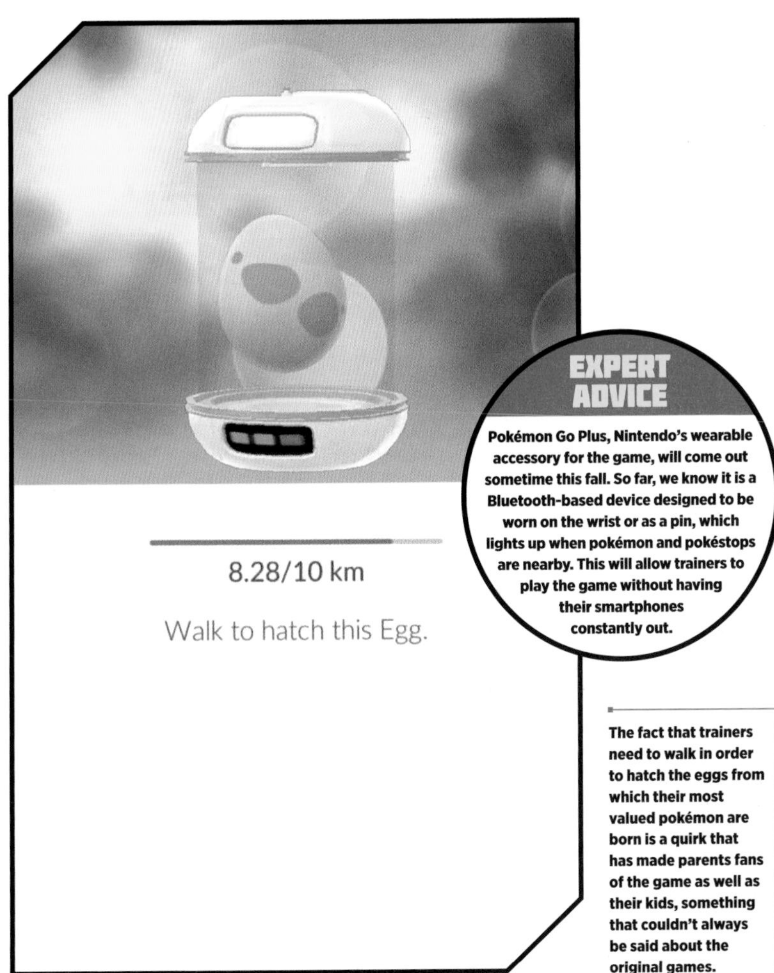

EXPERT ADVICE

Pokémon Go Plus, Nintendo's wearable accessory for the game, will come out sometime this fall. So far, we know it is a Bluetooth-based device designed to be worn on the wrist or as a pin, which lights up when pokémon and pokéstops are nearby. This will allow trainers to play the game without having their smartphones constantly out.

The fact that trainers need to walk in order to hatch the eggs from which their most valued pokémon are born is a quirk that has made parents fans of the game as well as their kids, something that couldn't always be said about the original games.

launch you to the game's most competitive levels in the shortest amount of time.

SEDENTARY EGG HATCHING

One facet of Pokémon Go that's been bringing smiles to cardiologists around the country is how the app forces trainers to walk long distances to hatch eggs into Exeggcutes. It's yet another great way to encourage people to explore their surroundings, a cornerstone of Pokémon Go's philosophy. It also can be a tremendous

Although there were earlier reports that schemes like taping your phone to a ceiling fan or resting it on a turntable would skip the necessity for actual physical work in Pokémon Go, those theories have since been debunked. Eggs have to be hatched honestly, so start walking it off.

EXPERT ADVICE

Still worried you won't ever be able to catch them all? If you look into Niantic's official terms of service for Pokémon Go, there's a section that specifically permits players to trade pokémon "characters or creatures" during gameplay, a definite hint of what's to come in later versions of the game.

and tedious time-suck, especially when you just want to see if that 10 km egg is going to hatch into a Lapras. Fortunately, intrepid trainers have discovered a variety of ways to log in the demanded distance without getting up from the couch.

- Enlist your real-life pet to help you hatch new, virtual pets. Pokémon Go calculates distance walked in a more-or-less straight line toward your incubating eggs, invalidating early rumors that trainers could just attach the phone to a turntable or ceiling fan and wait for a Jynx to appear. However, gently attaching your phone to a dog and letting him or her roam free in the house or in your backyard should rack up the kilometers while protecting you from the fresh air and socialization that many Pokémon Go players enjoy.

When a gym becomes white, it's up for grabs for anyone in the area, not just the trainers who may have put in the hard work to defeat that gym's pokémon.

• Everyone laughed at you when you bought a Roomba. They scoffed when you showed them your personal drone. But now your wildly impractical impulse purchases have become your path to lazy pokémon trainerdom. Securely attach your device to one of your expensive toys and have them go the distance for you.

SNIPE THOSE GYMS

While gym battles are framed as team vs. team affairs, the mechanics of how a gym is actually taken over allow for a third party with quick reflexes and a cutthroat attitude to swoop in and claim victory for him or herself. Hang out by a known gym held by a rival team (or your own) and wait for the gym's color to turn white, indicating its prestige has been knocked down to zero. Normally, the trainer who has taken the effort to battle the gym down would leave one of his

EXPERT ADVICE

Defending your recently won gyms against "snipers" takes a bit of strategy and a quick touch. I always make sure to have at least one fully healed pokémon left in my lineup after every battle. That way, as soon as the gym turns white, I can immediately station a defender without wasting the precious time it takes to grab potions.

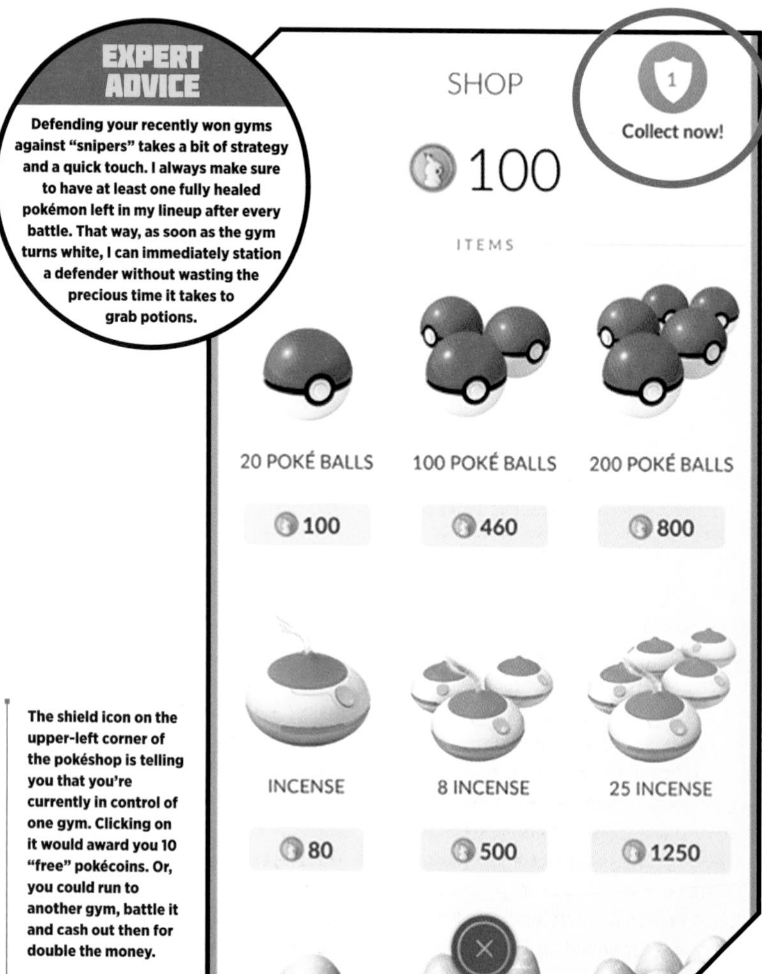

The shield icon on the upper-left corner of the pokéshop is telling you that you're currently in control of one gym. Clicking on it would award you 10 "free" pokécoins. Or, you could run to another gym, battle it and cash out then for double the money.

Knowing your history can be useful. The screen from "Ingress" (left) provides clues for the clever trainer in Pokémon Go.

or her pokémon to defend the hard-won prize. But if you are quick enough, you can tap on the white-colored gym and leave one of your pokémon there, just as if it were an unclaimed gym in the wild. Your options from here are either to try and rapidly build up that gym's level and make an effort at defending it from other trainers, or you can cash out for a quick 10 pokécoins, accepting your lone defender will be quickly overwhelmed by the multiple trainers in the area.

LEARN FROM HISTORY

Before bestowing Pokémon Go on the world, Niantic developed a similar augmented reality game called "Ingress." Like Pokémon Go, Ingress required players to explore the real world collecting virtual objects in a quest for victory. Veterans of "Ingress" now playing Pokémon Go have noticed that areas of the "Ingress" map with high concentrations of "XM" (which show up as white dots on the map) are fertile spawning grounds for pokémon. If you have the patience (and the battery power), running both of these apps provides a handy map for tracking down pokémon hotspots.

POKÉMANNERS

Pokémon Go is even more fun when everybody looks out for one another.

You can admit it now—you're hopelessly addicted to Pokémon Go. The good news is as long as you can manage to keep your common sense about you while playing, it's a fairly manageable dependence. In the rush to catch them all, it's understandable you want to grab as many pokémon in as short as time as possible. But in the process, it's important to follow these guidelines to keep yourself in good standing with friends, family and others you encounter on your journey to pokémon masterdom. After all, you can't brag to your friends about having the best collection of pokémon around if you lose all your friends in the process of catching them. Follow these simple dos and don'ts, and you'll be a well-respected pokémaster in no time.

DOs AND DON'Ts

DO: GET A BATTERY EXTENDER AND USE THE AR SETTING

This way, when you're staring at your phone looking for the last Bulbasaur you need to evolve one, you can see the people—or automobiles—that may block your path.

DON'T: LOSE SIGHT OF WHERE YOU ARE

That ubiquitous load screen isn't a joke: The horror stories about players walking into traffic or other dangerous scenarios are well-documented. Don't become another anecdote. No pokémon is worth life or limb, so take care of yourself.

DO: FREQUENT LOCAL BUSINESSES AND TRY TO DEFEND THEM AS GYMS

Many local businesses across the world love Pokémon Go for a very simple reason: Becoming a pokéstop increases the number of people hanging around.

DON'T: SIT IN A CAFÉ ALL DAY DRINKING WATER AND PLAYING POKÉMON GO.

If you're playing Pokémon Go in a private establishment rather than public land, make sure you actually patronize the establishment. Grab lunch or dinner or at least buy something while you get your game on.

One of the most common tactics used by businesses to lure players into their storefronts is creating and advertising stops in bars, restaurants and other public centers.

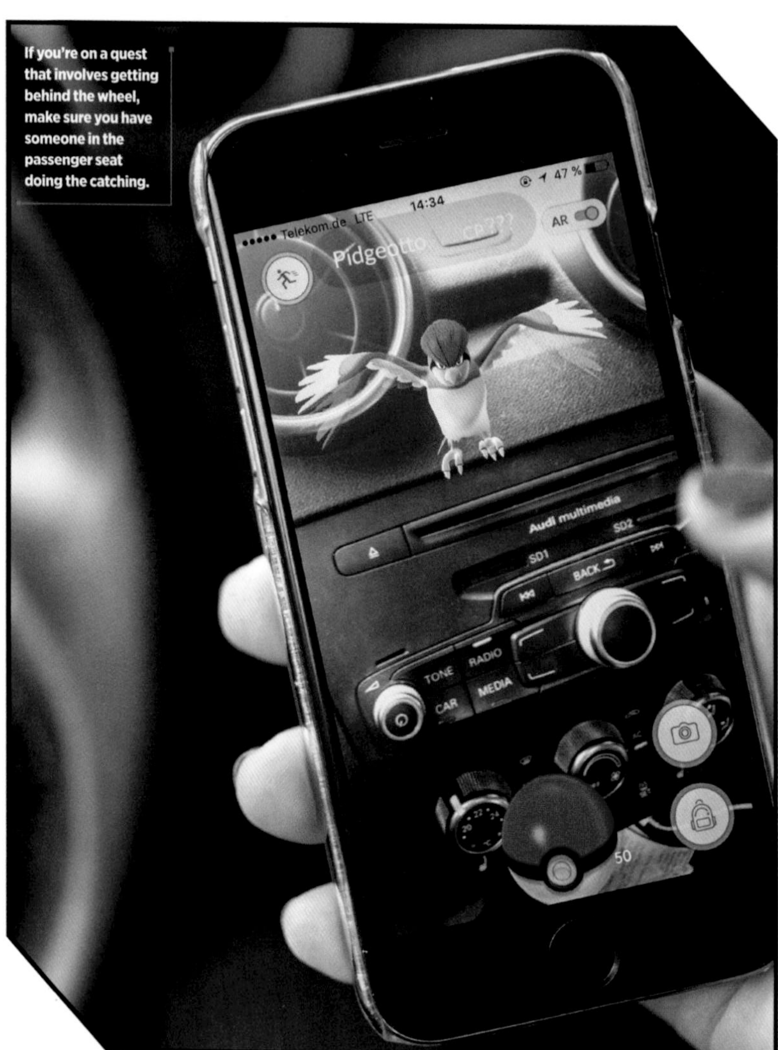

If you're on a quest that involves getting behind the wheel, make sure you have someone in the passenger seat doing the catching.

DO: PLAN HUNTS AROUND SPECIFIC AREAS AND DO A THOROUGH SWEEP

Working in teams is great, being thorough is better and covering every inch of ground is ideal. Plan a quick road trip to catch some pokémon you might not see in your neighborhood.

DON'T: HUNT AND DRIVE

Save the poké-search for after you've reached your agreed-upon destination. Attempting to catch and drive is worse than texting and driving, which is illegal in nearly every state.

DO: SHOW OFF YOUR POKÉ-WIT

One of the best things about the game is that you can name your pokémon whatever you like in order to separate and personalize them. Everybody gets a kick out of a good joke, especially one that can be shared with a community of like minds. So when you name your avatar "The Real Ash Ketchum" or "Omanyte of the Round Table," fellow players will respond with a chuckle. Of course, just pulling a funny moniker out of a baby name book is fun too, but less of a mental workout.

DON'T: SULLY THE GAME'S GOOD NAME

Pokémon has always been a game that has appealed both to children first learning video games and adults who enjoy the escapism of the pretend world. So keep your poké-nicknames PG for the sake of those around you.

DO: SHOW A LITTLE LOCAL PRIDE

When choosing your places to post up, give a little love to your local players, local gyms, local pokéstops, etc. Pokémon Go is one of the few things that can get neighbors in big cities to talk to each other.

DON'T: TURN IT INTO HOOLIGANISM

There have been reports of people using lures to isolate players and do them harm. It shouldn't even have to be said, but this is contrary to the spirit of the game and using poképowers for evil should result in a swift ban (and arrest).

EXPERT ADVICE

Before you add a pokémon to an allied gym, check to see which types your fellow trainers have put out for battle. A well-differentiated gym will be harder to beat than one that has multiple pokémon of the same type.

DO: EXPLORE NEW PLACES IN YOUR QUEST TO BE THE BEST

You never know what pokémon might be lurking by that new park that just opened nearby, or on trails as you switch up your daily jog. Try to cover as much ground as possible.

DON'T: FORGET YOUR MANNERS IN THE PROCESS

As has been shown by poké-quests spilling over into historically revered ground like the Holocaust Museum and Arlington National Cemetery, not every location is a good place to walk through screaming "There's a Tentacool!"

DO: HUNT IN PACKS

As a wise person once said, there's safety in numbers, and this is also true in the world of Pokémon Go. Bringing friends along will increase the number of newly spotted pokémon as well as add an interesting social aspect to the game.

DON'T: BETRAY YOUR OWN

There's no need to evolve into a champion rugby player as you dive like James Bond dodging a bullet so you can get a perfect curveball shot at that wild Dragonair. Look out for each other and share the wealth.

EXPERT ADVICE

Make sure you leave local parks and other public places before they close. Don't make the police work harder than they do already.

Pokémon Go meet-up groups have sprung up across the country, encouraging strangers to catch them all together.

DO: ENGAGE IN FRIENDLY COMPETITION

"How many did you catch today?" should be just about the extent of direct questions to a rival player. Pokémon Go is fun, and it's very easy to keep it that way if everyone keeps a cool head.

DON'T: LEAVE A FELLOW TRAINER BEHIND

Just because you've already caught a pokémon doesn't mean you should leave a fellow player to their own devices when they're trying to add it to their pokédex. It's just rude. Wait until all parties are ready to depart an area then head off together.

SMART SPENDING

So you're willing to pony up some real-life cash to help your Pokémon Go game? Here's how to get the most bang for your bucks.

Pokémon Go is by no means a pay-to-win game, so if you think you're going to become the top trainer in your city just by shelling out more cash than your neighbors, we're sorry. As of now, you can purchase only seven items in the pokéshop, many of which you can also easily obtain by leveling up or visiting pokéstops in the game. You'll need to first understand how buying items works before determining whether exchanging dead presidents for digital poké items makes sense for you.

Access the pokéshop by clicking on the pokéball icon on the bottom of your main map screen. The button is in the center of your screen right below the pokédex. Every item you can obtain in the store costs gold pokécoins, which you can either obtain by scrolling down to the bottom of the shop screen and purchasing with your own, real-world money or by cashing in on your gym bonus by clicking the shield icon on the upper-right-hand corner of the pokéshop page. Inside the shield icon, you will see a number marking how many pokémon you currently have defending gyms in the game. Once every 21 hours, you can press it and cash in on a defender bonus, which will give you 10 pokécoins for every pokémon you have stationed at a gym at the time. **You also get 100 free pokécoins at the beginning of the game (which you should use to buy pokéballs)** and, on rare occasions, the digital currency can also be collected from pokéstops.

However, Ponyta-ing up real money can give you some big advantages in the game if you use your pokécoins wisely. Here are four types of trainers and which items are best to shell out for depending on their strategy. Match your own style to these templates to determine which payment plan is right for you.

THE NOVICE

You've just started out in the game and need to catch up to your friends—fast. Your aim will probably be to level up as quickly as possible while making the pokémon swarm to you like Beedrills to honey. To best utilize your real-world money, stock up on **lucky eggs** (which will double your XP for 30 minutes), **incense** (which will make you super-attractive to pokémon for 30 minutes) and **lure modules**, which you can activate at pokéstops to attract higher numbers of stronger pokémon than you would normally see at a low level in the game. Use them all together, and you've got maximum pokémon-catching and leveling-up efficiency. You're welcome.

THE COLLECTOR

Is your aim to catch them all before any other trainer you know? You'll want to shell out some real money for extra egg incubators and a pokémon storage upgrade. **Egg incubators** in the pokéshop can only be used three times, so we recommend saving them to hatch 5km or 10km eggs and save your 2km eggs for the infinite incubator you automatically received in your bag at the beginning of the game. Eggs often hatch rarer, higher-level pokémon than you would normally find in the real world and can deliver critters that are otherwise uncommon in your area. So, with eggs, even someone living in Tempe could get a super-strong Lapras on deck. With the **pokémon storage upgrade**, you can stock up extra pokémon that you can turn into Professor Willow for extra candy and use to help evolve more pokémon, which will also help with your collecting. Currently, your poké-pocket is capped at 250 monsters, so if you're considering doing some serious pokémon farming, the extra space could be essential.

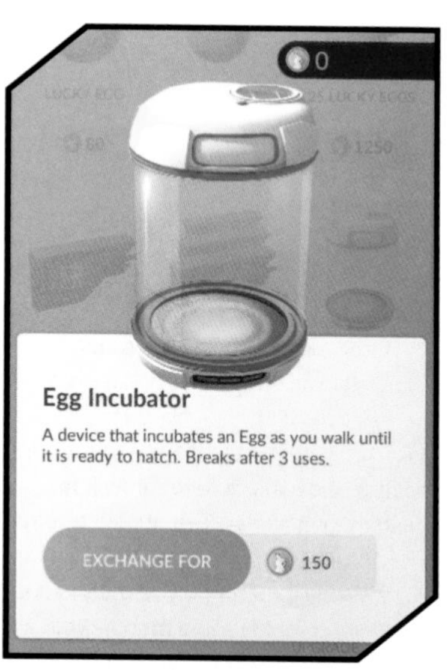

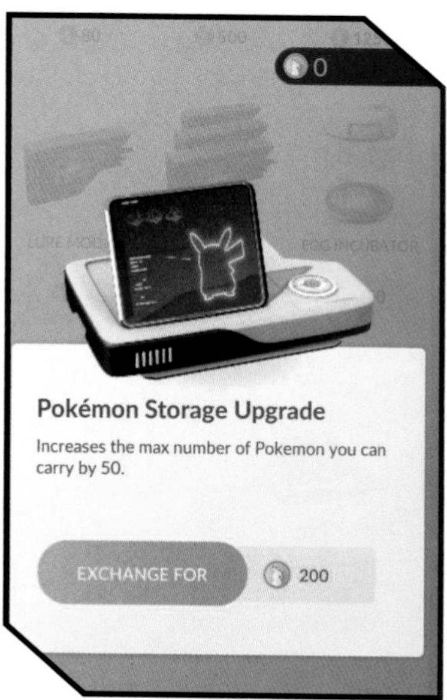

EXPERT ADVICE

Too broke to pay into the game? Mooch off of other people's good fortune by hunting in places like shopping malls, universities and other relatively high-income areas, where people aren't afraid to throw down for a lure module, and everyone can benefit.

THE COUCH POTATO

Really don't want to have to get up and walk 8km a day just to play Pokémon Go? Stuck in an office? Feeling sick and need to take a day off from training? Spend that sweet money by loading up on **pokéballs**, incense and lure modules. This way, you won't have to travel to pokéstops to snag the essential pokémon-traps, and the pokémon you want to catch will come to you. Just make sure you're sitting down in a place that has a pokéstop you can easily activate without moving, and make sure to throw lure modules on it all day. Team up with some friends for a lure party if you really want to get the most bang for your buck. Plus, when you combine a lure module with an incense, the only limit to your pokémon roundup is the money you're willing to spend. Make sure to stock up on extra pokéballs to keep up with all the catching.

THE BATTLE MASTER

If your plan is to take control of every gym in your neighborhood, you're going to need a bigger bag. Why? **The bag upgrade** will allow you to carry a lot more items, which you can use to stock up on potions to heal your wounded pokémon before an all-day attack. Unfortunately, you can't buy potions in the pokéshop, so you'll have to hit up a lot of pokéstops to save up on elixirs before you head into the fray. You also might want to stock up on some lucky eggs while you're preparing for battle. As we've noted before, trainer level is supreme when it comes to achieving max CP for your pokémon. You can use lucky eggs to help gain XP as quickly as possible, which will help you level up twice as fast.

TWENTY YEARS OF CATCHING THEM ALL

Pokémon Go is just the latest entry in a franchise that's been delighting generations of fans for two decades.

The breathtaking success of Pokémon Go may appear to have seized the world overnight, but its gestation began decades ago, with the childhood of the creator of these lovable creatures, Satoshi Tajiri. Tajiri grew up in a suburban area of Tokyo catching insects and tadpoles for fun, and as a video game designer he wanted to spread the joy he felt as an adventurous child. Tajiri came up with the idea of "capsule monsters," a pitch Nintendo was excited to develop starting in 1990. After changing the name to Pocket Monsters, which was conveniently shortened to Pokémon, Nintendo released the Game Boy games "Pokémon Red" and "Pokémon Green" to Japan on February 27, 1996. Though sales were modest at first, a popular Japanese magazine called *CoroCoro* held a contest offering to distribute the elusive legendary pokémon, Mew, to 20 entrants. The game's popularity skyrocketed as the contest received 78,000 entrants, and the new "Pokémon Blue" game swiftly followed as a companion to "Red" and "Green."

These games started with the 151 pokémon that are now available on the Pokémon Go app, and from the beginning the objective of the game has been to become a pokémon master by exploring different regions and collecting all the different types. The first set of Pokémon trading cards became an instant sensation after it was released in October 1996, and the following year in April, the beloved anime spinoff was born. The main character was named Satoshi after Pokémon's creator, later changed to Ash in the English version. In August 1997, the successful show inspired a manga called

EXPERT ADVICE

So far, Pokémon Go's hidden "easter eggs" seem to reference lore and story arcs established in the original anime series. If you're looking to discover rare pokémon, secret battle advantages or other game-related tweaks before the rest of your fellow pokétrainers, I'd recommend watching the show from start to finish and testing theories as you go.

The Pokémon trading card game, known in poké-circles as TCG, has printed more than 21 billion cards and laid the groundwork for the battle stats that power Pokémon Go.

In *Pokémon: The First Movie*, Mewtwo, the genetically engineered 150th pokemon, played the role of the villain. Opposite: On September 28, 1998, North America got its first taste of the Pokémon phenomenon with the release of "Pokémon Red" and "Blue."

Pokémon Adventures that, like the show, continues to thrive today. The exciting "Red" and "Blue" versions of the game and the anime made their way to North America in 1998, now with the iconic "Gotta Catch 'Em All!" slogan attached. The franchise's amazing sales in the United States underscored Pokémon's universal appeal and proved that the creatures were more than just a passing fad. The international release of the second version of "Pokémon Stadium" for the Nintendo 64, along with a feature film, pushed the franchise to new heights. The movie proved so popular in the U.S. it even held, for a period, the title of highest-grossing opening for an animated movie. The movie's astounding success was followed by "Pokémon Yellow," released in 1998 in Japan and 1999 in North America. This game, in conjunction with the anime, caused Pikachu to become the most widely recognized pokémon and treasured mascot of the franchise. Several spin-off games spanning genres made the craze available to children of all interests; for example, the popular "Pokémon Snap" released in 1999 allowed players to take pictures of pokémon, which were then graded on their quality by the now well-known Professor Oak.

The Game Boy games were still by far the most popular element of the Pokémon empire. "Gold" and "Silver" were released on the Game Boy Color in 1999 in Japan, adding 100 new pokémon, the capability to breed pokémon, a time system (the game's internal clock keeps track of time in the real-world, and certain events occur at specific times) and shiny pokémon to the games. "Pokémon Crystal," like "Yellow," was the improved third version from this generation of games, and it allowed trainers to choose the gender of their pokémon for the first time. The third generation of pokémon was introduced in 2003 with the release of "Ruby" and "Sapphire" to North America, this time on the Game Boy Advance. These games implemented battling, contests, and special abilities. The third version, "Emerald," was released in 2005, and together with the other two games became the bestselling Game Boy Advance games of all time. "Diamond" and "Pearl," released in 2007, introduced specific gender differences, a split between special and physical abilities and a new time system. They were joined by "Pokémon Platinum" two years later, though it was released on the Nintendo DS instead of the Advance. "Pokémon Black" and "White" introduced the largest addition of new pokémon yet (156), along with the first female pokémon expert—Professor Araragi. Set in Unova, an area based on New York City, this game was the first to be based in the United States instead of Japan, underscoring how the franchise truly belonged to the world.

Nineteen movies, 17 seasons of anime and countless manga later, Pokémon continues to inspire the imaginations of

Pokémon Kanto Monopoly, which replaces the traditional Atlantic City landmarks with pokémon-centric items, was released in 2014 after years of makeshift fan versions.

Pokémon: The First Movie was the highest-grossing film based on a video game until the 2001 release of *Lara Croft: Tomb Raider*.

both children and adults in every corner of the globe. That's why players around the world continue to trade, battle and explore in the ever-expanding Pokémon universe. The adventurous attitude Satoshi hoped to instill in players has grown and manifested into a timeless movement. And now, for the first time, the cute creatures have come to our world through the mobile app Pokémon Go, which, with the help of augmented reality, allows players to catch pokémon in their own homes, schools, offices and more. No matter where these new trainers live, the app encourages them to get off the couch and live out the fantasy many have harbored since childhood, and no doubt ensures pokéfever will continue to stick around for decades to come.

While Pokémon Go is being embraced by players of all ages, the nostalgia factor particularly appeals to millennials, such as this group of young people at a lure gathering in London.

BRINGING EVERYONE TOGETHER

While hunting for pokémon, millions of trainers have found a community.

A LITTLE POKÉMIRACLE

Like so many other Pokémon Go users, Kaitlin Kouts and Tiffany Revay were exploring and searching for wild pokémon in their neighborhood park in Lufkin, Texas. The two had ordered pizza, and while they waited for it to arrive, Kouts added a Jigglypuff to her pokédex. She was looking to see if there were any more hanging around, when she spotted a puppy near a tree.

"Instead of a Jigglypuff, I found a puppy," Kouts told KTRE. "The puppy was lying by the tree in a trash bag and could not move. His mouth was bleeding; he wasn't moving very much. He looked like he was in pain. We found out his back leg was broken. His gums were pale and blue and so were his ears."

While trying to figure out where the puppy had come from, the girls got a call from a pizza delivery man, Skyler Jerke, saying that he had arrived with their food. They explained the situation to him, and Jerke, also an EMT, was more than happy to help. The hurt puppy was taken to the hospital, treated for his injuries and named Pokey, after the game that had helped save his life.

KEEPING SPIRITS HIGH

The quest to catch them all is adding a little joy to the days of children staying in a Michigan children's hospital. Before the release of Pokémon Go, the patients at C.S. Mott Children's Hospital would "shuffle" around the hospital with their heads down, not speaking to one another. But now that the popular app has united the kids with a common interest, they walk together through

EXPERT ADVICE

You've probably been waiting to use the line "I choose you" for a while now, and this is the perfect time to drop it without seeming weird. Plus, getting to know someone over a common hobby that encourages you to explore your area far outshines a humdrum "Netflix and chill" session. And because Pokémon Go is free, it's one of the cheapest ways to go out!

the halls catching Pokémon and crowd around pokéstops talking to each other about their latest catch.

"It's a fun way to encourage patients to be mobile," says J.J. Bouchard, a child life specialist for the hospital. "This app is getting patients out of beds and moving around." According to Bouchard, there are multiple pokéstops in the hospital as well as a gym positioned in front of a Big Bird statue. Beyond battling and collecting items, he says children even help each other pose with their favorite pokémon for pictures.

FINDING LOVE IN AN AR WORLD

If you enjoy catching pokémon on the weekend more than going to bars, a new Pokémon Go dating app called Pokématch may be for you. Co-developers Rene Roosen and Pim de Witte came up with the idea for the app when their friends complained of wanting a date that was as into pokémon hunting as they are. The two wasted no time developing and releasing the app under guidance of famous entrepreneur Troy Osinoff. "When an idea like this comes by, you just have to be the first to build it and release it. The style updates and fixes can come later. People need this now," says de Witte.

Besides being an easy icebreaker, Pokémon Go allows people to explore their cities while getting to know each other, creating deeper connections between Pokémon fanatics everywhere.

The app works much like many other dating apps, and as of yet doesn't have the pokéstops integrated into the map design. But Osinoff is happy with the familiar design and hopeful future updates will be able to integrate the map features. "We're taking a familiar approach to dating and applying it to the poké-world," says Osinoff "Our goal is to help everyone find their Brock or Misty."

From left: The logo for Pokématch, a dating site promising to bring together romantically compatible trainers; a pair of trainers at Retiro Park in Madrid, Spain.

A restaurant in Canterbury, U.K., advertises itself as a location for rare pokémon. The game, which was rolled out in the U.K. on July 14, has proved just as popular as in America.

ROLLING IN IT

Local businesses are cashing in on the Pokémon craze.

The streets of cities all over the world teeming with Pokémon Go gamers undergoing long treks to complete their pokédex, and businesses are luring customers (in more ways than one) into their restaurants, bars and boutiques with the promise of pokémon. Some establishments got lucky; they're located within range of a pokéstop or gym. It's natural for app users to sit down, order some merchandise and hang out for a brief break, and businesses are looking to capitalize on the new influx of potential customers any way they can.

A grilled cheese shop in Medford, New Jersey, started a promotion for Pokémon Go users who bought an entree in their restaurant. They began giving out free ice cream, which went a lot better than they had previously anticipated. "We are waiting for an ice cream truck right now," Sam Daly, the Pop Shop's restaurant manager, told CBS News. "We are almost out of ice cream. As soon as the truck gets here, we will be very happy." A bar and restaurant called CitySen Lounge in Grand Rapids, Michigan, had similar luck. They posted a pokémon-related sign outside the restaurant, which not unlike in-game incense, drew pokémon hunters straight to their establishment.

EXPERT ADVICE

If Pokémon Go players are short on anything, it's battery life. If you're looking for business, offer up some outlets to weary trainers or stock up on some extra chargers from your local electronics store to help give potential customers a boost. Offering refreshments or special discounts also wouldn't hurt!

McDonald's became the first major brand name to capitalize on the Pokémon Go phenomenon when they paid for the privilege of making 3,000 of its Japanese locations double as gyms in the game. "it is a global phenomenom, clearly," McDonald's CEO Steve Easterbrook said on a July 26 investor call.

"This weekend, we were just people-watching and noticed everybody staring at their phones," John Merritt, manager of CitySen Lounge, said to *Adweek*. "So, we put the sign up... the sign alone brought in some foot-traffic." Merritt is thinking about setting up a lure in CitySen to entice even more hungry app-users into the restaurant. This increase in customers has some businesses wanting to establish gyms or pokéstops outside their establishments.

EXPERT ADVICE

Yelp created a filter for Pokémon Go players to use to help find businesses with pokéstops and gyms nearby. Google Maps also has specially designated Pokémon Go maps that let people know which pokémon are likely to be found near certain locations. Or, try linking up with others at poké bar crawls or group hunts to get a lay of the land.

Playing during off-hours like at night can ensure you get onto the server and increase your chances of evolving that Spearow into a Fearow.

Although the placement of pokéstops and gyms has thus far been random, Niantic's CEO John Hanke confirmed that sponsored locations are coming to Pokémon Go and businesses can apply to be a pokéstop or gym through Niantic's website. Fast food giant McDonald's has reaped the benefit of increased sales thanks to a deal it struck transforming 3,000 of its Japanese locations into gyms.

Meanwhile, Nintendo is not so lucky. It seems like the corporation that created Pokémon in the '90s is the only one not benefiting from it. The corporation's stock had a momentary rise but has since plummeted with the news that Nintendo didn't actually create the Pokémon Go app and was merely a licensor. In fact, Macquarie Securities analyst David Gibson told *Bloomberg* that he estimated Nintendo owned just 13 percent of the app. On the other hand, Niantic is was worth more than $3 billion within a month of the app's release.

STAR TRAINERS

They may have a massive amount of fame and fortune, but what these celebrities really crave are pokémon.

JIMMY FALLON

The Tonight Show host was one of the first celebrities to jump on the pokémon bandwagon within days of the app's release. He set up a lure to a pokéstop outside his house and found through the course of the night about 100 kids stopped by to take advantage of the active pokéstop. Unfortunately for Fallon, it seems like he only caught Zubats, a problem many players—talk show hosts included—experience.

Fallon and his late night colleagues found comedic gold in Pokémon Go. On *The Tonight Show,* Fallon poked fun at cops who stop trainers while driving. "The officials just drive ahead of them to catch all the pokémon. 'SUCKERS!'"

Hunting for pokémon in places like Central Park, where lots of other trainers are present, is great strategy. Much rarer pokémon than you'd normally see tend to appear near pokéstops that are highly populated. Plus, you're likely to run across tons of lit up lure modules, which attract much higher numbers than you'd see normally in the wild.

During his pokéquest around Manhattan, Justin Bieber went to Central Park and the Apple Store, both the sites of large gatherings of pokémon.

JUSTIN BIEBER

The young popstar was in NYC for his *Purpose* tour and decided to see what pokémon the Big Apple had to offer. On the evening of July 17, he went to Central Park with friend Alfredo Flores in tow, and the pair joined hundreds of other big-city trainers to track down the elusive pocket monsters. But the Biebs wasn't the biggest attraction that night. That honor belonged to the Gyarados rumored to be hiding in the park, and Bieber raced with hundreds of other app users to try to catch it. The singer was probably happy he wasn't the one being chased for once.

Chrissy Teigen has a love-hate relationship with the game, which she details in her Twitter feed. Addicted to gameplay, she faced the common problem of having pokémon get in the way of real life.

EXPERT ADVICE

Traveling around a lot can actually give aspiring pokémon masters a distinct advantage in the game. Certain monsters like Tauros, Farfetch'd and Mr. Mime are only common on certain continents. Plus, traveling exposes you to a multitude of diverse biomes, which attract different types of pokémon. Cross-country road trip anyone?

CHRISSY TEIGEN

The model, cookbook author, mother and Mrs. John Legend was at first skeptical of dipping her toes in the Pokémon Go pool. Before downloading the app, she asked her Twitter followers whether she was too old to play and wondered if it suited her jet setting, international lifestyle. Soon enough, like many other 30-year-olds who grew up watching Ash and Pikachu every week on the TV, nostalgia got the better of her and she started playing. She didn't even need to venture into the outside world to catch some pokémon. While watching a scene from the TV show *The Office*, a Venonat interrupted her viewing, which she tweeted to her adoring public.

On July 14 an unsuspecting *Daily Show* fan got the surprise of a lifetime when she ran directly into Trevor Noah while hunting for a Pidgey in New York.

TREVOR NOAH

The host of *The Daily Show* shared the frustration of trainers everywhere wrestling with the game's overloaded servers during its first few weeks on the market. He took to Twitter to complain about the servers as Niantic continued its plan to roll out the game in more countries, tweeting "So excited for Canada and Europe getting #PokemonGO. Now we can all share in our disdain of the @NianticLabs servers." But like any dedicated player, Noah persisted in his quest to catch them all and even shared a photo of his encounter with a wild Jynx.

JOE JONAS

The former (but technically still current) Jonas Brother, now the lead singer for DNCE, took a break from a delicious meal to catch a pokémon many consider cute enough to eat—Pikachu. He took advantage of a new locale and spent his vacation in Mexico hunting for pokémon. The singer is clearly a big believer in finding pokémon in different regions. He also suggested on Twitter that Mewtwo might be sequestered in Area 51, tweeting "Rumor has it Mew2 is at Area 51... Road trip anyone? #PokemonGO." Of course as a responsible trainer, Jonas knows better than to trespass while hunting for pokémon, particularly at military installations that may or may not contain aliens. You should definitely follow his lead.

A SHINY NEW REALITY

Pokémon Go is the beginning of a new normal for gaming, but where will this new technology lead?

Right now, the concept of augmented reality—the superimposing of a user interface or fictional world over the real one through the use of a smartphone or eyewear like Google Glass—has found a solid niche in the "Gotta Catch 'Em All" world. The ability to seek pokémon out in a familiar environment while being able to toss a genuine pokéball at them has proved a powerful draw for new fans of the game and nostalgic grown-ups alike, and Pokémon Go has introduced all of its millions of players to the concept of augmented reality in a way that might see the technology branch out in the near future to include an entirely augmented existence. This will change the way we play games, as has already been proven, but it can also change the way we travel and the way we interact with those around us—including even the way we buy groceries.

In May 2016, a filmmaker and design professional named Keiichi Matsuda made a beautiful, jarring and at times eerie six-minute film depicting a day in the life of a Medellin, Colombia, woman set in a future where augmented reality has taken a prime place in gaming, advertising, internet activity and commerce. Walking down the street, the woman passes a blogger and the blogger's homepage and username pop up in a comic book thought cloud above their head. Even unmarked taxis are conveniently identifiable by the digital word "Taxi" along their sides in giant letters. At the supermarket, a digital dog follows her around pointing out specials and other discounts. The plethora of colors and moving shapes is stunning, but it's the possibilities that really blow the minds of casual observers: Foreign-language street signs would no longer be indecipherable to travelers and new-arrivals; stopping for directions would become a thing of the past; overpaying for even the most trivial item would be next to impossible. But the most ubiquitous truths are becoming clear as gaming makes the first breach in the augmented reality wall—there will be more fun had by more people, more

EXPERT ADVICE

Heads up digital purists: Pokémon Go isn't quite "true" augmented reality, which requires computer vision and dynamic mapping of real-world environments. So far, players must still rely solely on Google Maps' fixed latitude and longitude, instead of the real-time depth mapping and object recognition required for full-blown AR.

For gamers hoping to have a more traditional pokémon catching experience—or just save their battery life—it is possible to turn AR mode off and replace your surroundings with a generic pokémon scene.

exercise to be disguised as gameplay and more community building in the real world as well as the digital realm thanks to the world on top of a world concept of AR gaming.

The phenomenon began in earnest in 2012 with the game "Ingress," created by Niantic, who would later be responsible for Pokémon Go. In "Ingress," players used a basic AR format to take control of various monuments and landmarks by claiming "portals." This concept has reached its adulthood with the more child-friendly Pokémon Go, but there are still plenty of trails to be blazed in the relatively new world of AR gaming. Many of them could lead to breakthroughs that change the way we interact with the real world as a whole, from education to logistics to surviving that post-college backpack trip with your wallet and your pride in one piece. Already, AR apps are revolutionizing the way users interact with and discover their world. Through an app called Field Trip, curious wanderers, travelers, bored passengers on long road trips and history buffs of all shapes and sizes can be alerted to historic sites and places of note. Star Walk, another app, helpfully divides the night sky into recognizable constellations, making astronomy as easy as reading (kind of).

What is beginning as a fairly simple enterprise of gaming and trivia, according to Jonathon Narvey in his

Betakit article "Pokémon Go Takes us Back to Future of Augmented Reality," will become much more: "We could be on the verge of experiencing truly immersive environments that can help us forge new experiences, navigate difficult decisions and even imagine what it would be like to live in alternate realities." In short, playing Pokémon Go could be practice for a fully integrated future in which our very reality is defined by what our devices make of it. All the more reason to keep catching them all.

EXPERT ADVICE

Can't get enough of AR? Once you're done tracking down Pikachus in the wild, check out games like "SpecTrek," where you hunt ghosts instead of pocket monsters, or "Warp Runner," a puzzle game that turns any flat surface into a playing platform. Also, keep an eye out for copycat games that are bound to be coming out soon.

This Ryhorn in the middle of the street illustrates a possible danger of AR games—people so engrossed in the virtual world that they ignore real-world danger.